THE REFERENCE SHELF VOLUME 45 NUMBER 4

REPRESENTATIVE AMERICAN SPEECHES: 1972-1973

EDITED BY WALDO W. BRADEN

Professor of Speech
Louisiana State University

THE H. W. WILSON COMPANY
NEW YORK 1973

THE REFERENCE SHELF

The books in this series contain reprints of articles, excerpts from books, and addresses on current issues and social trends in the United States and other countries. There are six separately bound numbers in each volume, all of which are generally published in the same calendar year. One number is a collection of recent speeches; each of the others is devoted to a single subject and gives background information and discussion from various points of view, concluding with a comprehensive bibliography. Books in the series may be purchased individually or on subscription.

International Standard Book Number 0-8242-0507-3

Library of Congress Catalog Card Number (38-27962)

PRINTED IN THE UNITED STATES OF AMERICA

PREFACE

During the past year speakers have had many opportunities to express themselves. At the two major political conventions which met six weeks apart in Miami in the summer of 1972, politicians filled the air with all manner of polemics. However, about all that can be said for them is that they put on good shows but little more.

In early July the Democrats led off with what proved to be an undisciplined rumble. More than 80 percent of the delegates had never before attended a national convention; 38 percent were women and 15 percent were blacks. Some of the most exciting exchanges, particularly the platform debates dealing with abortion and homosexuality, occurred in the late hours after many television viewers, exhausted by the endless happenings, had gone to bed. Yvonne Braithwaite Burke, a young black chairwoman, won admiration for her dignity and tact in presiding over the endless roll calls. Among the better speeches were Senator Edward M. Kennedy's unity speech (probably written by Richard Goodwin), a speech described by *Newsweek* as "a short and generous stem winder," and Senator George S. McGovern's acceptance speech. It was a dramatic moment when Mike Gravel, senator from Alaska and one of eighty nominees for the vice presidency, "elbowed his way onto the rostrum, to second his own candidacy." At the end it seemed anticlimactic and not too genuine when the five erstwhile competitors for the presidential nomination, after vehemently castigating each other, stood together on the platform with linked hands raised and smiled to the cheering delegates.

Having witnessed the endless Democratic maneuverings, the Republicans resolved to stage a better show that would emphasize their unity in supporting the Nixon-Agnew team; consequently, they indulged in little extemporaneous debate, few dramatic moments, and little deviation from the time schedule. The proceedings as a whole seemed staid. Perhaps one writer was right to suggest that the convention had "the aura of a jubilant coronation." (Max Frankel, New York *Times,* August 27, 1972) *Newsweek* thought that President Nixon's acceptance speech had a "graver, more magisterial note in the delivery" than his first inaugural had had four years earlier (September 4, 1973, page 18). But even a greater contrast was noticed in the Vice President, who now was referred to as "a new and soft-spoken Spiro Agnew." (New York *Times,* August 27, 1972) He gave up "the partisan and personal attacks" and substituted "in their place . . . a modest little civics lesson on the nature of the vice presidency." (*Newsweek,* September 4, 1972)

Soon getting under way in September, the campaign provided little real clash between the two major antagonists. On September 3, 1972, Nixon kicked off the Republican campaign with a Labor Day speech from San Clemente, California, over nationwide radio. He determined that he could "best campaign by not campaigning." Claiming that he was too busy with matters of state to indulge in stumping, the President sent into the field over three dozen "surrogates," including members of the cabinet, White House staff, prominent senators and representatives, governors, friends, and even his wife, his daughters, and a brother (New York *Times,* September 6, 1972). To help "a few close friends among senatorial candidates," as November approached he traveled by motorcade through ten states with large electoral votes, generally engaging in "no rallies, no speeches, no news conferences, only the ceremonial itself." Any speeches that he chanced to make had little significance (R. W. Apple, Jr., New York *Times,* November 1, 1972). As the election neared, he delivered a dozen "quiet" radio talks and only two addresses on television. It is interesting to note that the President turned more often to radio than television to reach the people.

Perhaps looking forward to 1976, Vice President Agnew, trim and bronzed, continued to promote his new image. Tempering "the flamboyant rhetoric of his earlier campaigns" and "more attuned to issues, less to personalities," he explained that he was "trying to adopt a new style . . . that will not bring about . . . misconstructions in my intent." (Walter R. Mears (AP), Baton Rouge *State Times*, September 9, 1972) Dropping "his old shrillness in favor of a more judicious, lighthearted and confident style," Agnew covered thirty-two states and more than 35,000 miles (*Time*, November 6, 1972, page 44). One writer thought that his voice lacked "boom and resonance" and that his start was "always more lively than the middle or ending." (Courtney R. Sheldon, *The Christian Science Monitor*, September 22, 1972)

George McGovern and his wife took to the hustings with energy and righteous indignation. Selected as vice presidential candidate after Eagleton had stepped down, Sargent Shriver added his skill and pursued the voters, long and hard. On many occasions he appeared more effective and aggressive than his running mate. "Shriver, oddly, often comes across almost as bombastic as the old Agnew," said one writer; "yet there is an ebullience about him that makes him the liveliest of the top four candidates." (*Time*, November 6, 1972, page 44) Senator McGovern made numerous trips across the country, appeared frequently on television, and employed many spot commercials. Warren Weaver, Jr., (New York *Times*, October 22, 1972) commented: "The 1972 campaign, more than any other, is taking place on television and radio, in the newspapers, and in the mail—both through news accounts of the ritual political events and through direct paid messages for and against the candidates. For the great majority of Americans, the media are the campaign."

The handling of the Democratic vice presidential debacle, the President's refusal to discuss the Watergate break-in immediately after it occurred, and the Administration's success in cooling down the war in Vietnam left George McGovern in an awkward position. Noting the Democratic nominee's frustration, Godfrey Sperling (*The Christian Science Monitor,* November 31, 1972) declared that he could recall no other presidential candidate "at least in this century" who "held such deep-seated antagonism for, and complete distrust of, his opponent." It was observed that McGovern "turned more furiously evangelical than any major-party candidate since William Jennings Bryan . . . [returning] more and more to the old moral absolutes—and to the harshest rhetoric of any campaign in memory" (Peter Goldman and Richard Stout, *Newsweek,* November 6, 1972, page 43). In spite of his rage, the South Dakota senator did not stir President Nixon to take the platform or even reply. Perhaps there was truth in the editorial in *The Christian Science Monitor* (November 2, 1972) that said: "Senator McGovern's greatest failing with today's electorate is his candor. President Nixon's great strength is non-candor."

The following editorial from *The Christian Science Monitor* (November 2, 1972) sums up the campaign:

> No one can say that the speeches made during the American presidential campaign of 1972 have added substantially to public understanding of national problems, national issues or national means. There has been more obscuring than identifying; more vilifying than enlightening. The appeal has been to emotion rather than to reason.

Lamenting the absence of vigorous debate, Roscoe Drummond thought the whole affair was "dull, desultory, inanimate." (*The Christian Science Monitor,* November 13, 1972) In the end, President Nixon won by the greatest landslide in history.

In addition to the presidential race, in eighteen states gubernatorial contests were waged. One third of the senators were up for reelection with dramatic contests occurring in North Carolina, Alabama, Georgia, Illinois, Michigan, South Dakota, Rhode Island, New Mexico, and Oregon (*Time,* November 6, 1972). The Women's Political Caucus indicated that thirty-four women ran for Congress on the tickets of the two major parties, ten as Republicans and twenty-four as Democrats. An additional twenty-five women ran on minor-party tickets.

During the past twelve months, the formal speaking efforts of President Nixon have been minimal. Choosing means other than public address, he has communicated with the American people through his press secretary and aides, much to the dismay of reporters and critics eager to confront the President directly on vital issues. His more important speeches have been largely ceremonial in nature. Perhaps one of his most dramatic addresses was delivered in Moscow via radio and television, May 28, 1972, to the people of the Soviet Union. Upon his return from Europe he gave an equally stimulating address to a joint session of the Senate and the House of Representatives on the evening of June 1, 1972. Other important ceremonial speeches included his acceptance speech at the National Republican Convention, August 29, 1972; his brief victory speech on November 7, 1972; and his Second Inaugural Address delivered January 20, 1973.

Breaking with recent practice, the President chose not to submit a single State of the Union address, but to forward to Congress "several messages on individual topics to permit more careful consideration of the challenges we face." With each part, he presented a speech via radio to the public, explaining and defending his views.

The President gave an interesting speech to the South Carolina legislature, February 20, 1973, on the meaning of the settlement in Vietnam or what he termed "peace with honor." He felt comfortable on this occasion because he was addressing the first state legislature in the nation which "passed a resolution supporting the peace settlement." Not as polished as some of his other efforts (for example the speech to the Russian people), the South Carolina speech probably is representative of Nixon's own style because he spoke without notes and largely without the help of the usual ghost writers.

On March 29, 1973, at 9:00 P.M. President Nixon gave his first major policy speech of his new term over the television and radio networks. On this occasion he dealt with the war in Vietnam, rising food prices, and the budget crisis. The speech stirred the Democrats to designate Senator Edmund Muskie of Maine to respond, but the networks refused to grant equal time to the senator (see *Congressional Record*, April 13, 1973, page S6392).

By far the President's most impassioned speech was the one he delivered April 30, 1973, concerning the Watergate affair. Because of its intensity and dramatic qualities the speech is presented in this volume.

In reading the *Congressional Record*, day after day, the critic may ponder why so many of the speeches actually delivered on the floor of Congress are so pedestrian. Why are there no Borahs, La Follettes, Tafts, or even a Huey P. Long of yesteryear? Why are there so few good speeches by such capable speakers as Frank Church, Hubert Humphrey, Edward M. Kennedy, Mark O. Hatfield, Edward Brooke, or Margaret Chase Smith? Remembering that the printing cost of a single page of the *Record* is $163 and that transcription of proceedings requires sixteen shorthand reporters, the reader may further inquire why so much drivel—newspaper articles, editorials, essays of high school students, sermons from a favorite pastor, little tidbits on miscellaneous topics—appears in the *Record*. Perhaps the answer is suggested in the reflections of freshman Senator James L. Buckley of New York. He explains:

> I was struck by the number of extracurricular demands on a senator's time, especially one who lives as close to millions of constituents as does a senator from New York: invitations to speak which for one good reason or another cannot be declined, ceremonial visits, people with problems whom one must see and cannot refer to staff, people in the Federal Government to get to know, and so on. The day begins to be splintered into all kinds of pieces even before the business of legislative work begins.

One thing that in my innocence I had not anticipated was the intensely political atmosphere that prevails within the Senate, the great impact of purely political considerations on specific actions taken by individual senators.

During 1972-1973, politically and rhetorically, women have made an impressive mark in the public forum. The two most influential groups were the National Organization for Women (NOW) with 400 chapters and 35,000 members and the National Women's Political Caucus (NWPC) which is organized in 50 states and has about 30,000 individual members. The latter organization attracted 1,300 to its first national convention in Houston, February 8-10, 1972. Speakers included Frances (Cissy) Farenthold, Elizabeth (Liz) Carpenter, Bella Abzug, and Patricia Schroeder. Two of the speeches delivered at this occasion are presented in this volume: one by Representative Shirley Chisholm and the second by Representative Schroeder.

In politics women were more visible than in the previous year. CBS's "Meet the Press" program of September 10, 1972, on which Gloria Steinem and Jill Ruckelshaus were interviewed, provides insight into the aspirations of women in politics. Frances Farenthold (Republican) won 46 percent of the vote in a runoff election for governor in Texas. In the fall elections women made only "modest" gains (New York *Times*, November 9, 1972). Winning seats for the first time were Elizabeth Holtzman (Democrat, New York), Patricia Schroeder (Democrat, Colorado), and Marjorie Holt (Republican, Maryland) and two blacks, Yvonne Braithwaite Burke (Democrat, California), and Barbara Jordan (Democrat, Texas). Another black woman, Cardiss Collins (Democrat, Illinois), won a special election in June 1973, bringing the total now in the House to fifteen. At age seventy-four, Republican Senator Margaret Chase Smith of Maine was defeated, leaving the Senate once again an exclusive men's club. In New York three women (all Democrats), were elected to the state Senate, and three (two Republicans and a Democrat) were sent to the state Assembly. In Connecticut seventeen, a decrease of three from the previous term, were returned to the state legislature.

Anne Armstrong of Texas became Counselor for Women's Programs, a position considered to be of cabinet rank, and Jill Ruckelshaus, wife of the acting director of the FBI, became her special assistant and a member of the White House staff.

Feminist groups across the country have turned to the group procedure called "consciousness raising," a kind of group therapy. Eight to twelve women meet in C-R groups to exchange views on their feelings "about themselves, each other, their husbands, their lovers, and women in general and men in general." They hope to gain a better understanding of themselves in order to gain respect for themselves and to "give them courage to fight for equality in a 'man's world.' " (Diana Loercher, *The Christian Science Monitor,* April 4, 1973)

Of greatest concern to feminist groups was their effort to gain passage of the equal rights amendment. At the time of this writing twenty-eight states have ratified the proposal, ten short of the needed number. Proponents have until March 1979 to get the necessary number for final acceptance. Indicative of pro and con in this struggle was a program on ABC's "Issues and Answers," broadcast February 25, 1973.

As in past years, lecturing has provided opportunities for speakers to earn considerable sums of money. Known as "the conscience of the Senate," Margaret Chase Smith, while she was in the Senate, criticized her colleagues for their poor attendance and suggested that they found the lecture fees more attractive than the public business. Revealed figures of income from speaking now gives credence to the former Maine senator's charges. In listing his net worth for campaign purposes, George McGovern admitted, "In the past five years my income from speaking has been higher every year than my Senate salary." He revealed that in 1969 he had earned $63,000 from speaking and writing. In 1971 Hubert

Humphrey received $83,150 in speech fees, twice as much as any of his colleagues. Receiving $2,000 per speech, the Minnesota senator spoke to such trade groups as insurance agents, dairymen, grocers, druggists, and electrical contractors, as well as to college groups. Oregon Senator Mark O. Hatfield earned $39,388. Senator James L. Buckley of New York received $15,663 for seven speeches, six of which were to Republican organizations in Indiana, California, and Florida. The Associated Milk Producers, a twenty-state dairymen's organization, topped the list of special interests that demonstrated a fondness for the oratory of congressmen, according to James R. Polk of the Washington *Star.* (St. Louis *Post Dispatch,* May 24, 1972) It is, of course, obvious that trade associations and political groups may have supported a favorite with a handsome speaking honorarium for past favors and future considerations. It is probably also true that several congressmen could not have maintained themselves in Washington without their outside income from writing and speaking.

On the other hand, more than half of the paid speaking appearances of congressmen were on college campuses. Wooster College paid Republican Senator Jacob K. Javits of New York $2,000 for a presentation. The University of Vermont and Indiana State University each gave $2,000 to Democratic Senator Abraham A. Ribicoff of Connecticut (New York *Times,* May 20, 1972). Other public figures have earned similar fees. For his participation in debate at William and Mary College, William F. Buckley received $2,500, while his opponent Ramsey Clark drew $1,500. The lecture platform continues to pay handsomely for those who attract attention.

As editor, I know better than anyone else that the completion of each annual volume of REPRESENTATIVE AMERICAN SPEECHES would be most difficult without the aid and advice of others. Many persons have supplied me with speech texts and background material. My friends and colleagues have generously assisted me. Loren Reid of the University of Missouri, David Cornell of Davidson College, and Ota Reynolds of Hunter College have called my attention to speeches that I would otherwise have overlooked. In my own department at Louisiana State University, Clinton Bradford, Stephen Cooper, Francine Merritt, Harold Mixon, and Owen Peterson have given me valuable comments about speeches and have supplied encouragement when it was needed. In addition to reviewing speeches, Barbara Walsh has assisted in the preparation of biographies. Most useful were the evaluations that I received from the members of Speech 58H, Contemporary Public Address, taught at Louisiana State University by Owen Peterson. My secretaries, Linda Klug, Annette Hathorn, and Rita Jensen, have been efficient and helpful.

WALDO W. BRADEN

Baton Rouge, Louisiana
July 1973

CONTENTS

THE SIXTIES: LYNDON BAINES JOHNSON REMEMBERED

MANAGEMENT OF NATURE

VIEWS ON EDUCATION

INAUGURATION: TWO VIEWS OF THE FUTURE

SECOND INAUGURAL ADDRESS [1]

RICHARD M. NIXON [2]

The Inauguration Celebration of January 20, 1973, was one of the most elaborate in history, costing some $4 million in contrast to $526 spent by Franklin D. Roosevelt for his fourth inauguration in 1945. The parade included hundreds of horses, thirty-odd floats, and numerous bands. Fifty thousand invitations had been sent to supporters. Two hundred thousand spectators lined the parade route. But the gaiety and the elaborateness of the planning could not mask the tenseness that prevailed throughout Washington. Thousands came to protest the Vietnam war and the conservative policies of the Nixon Administration. Some liberal congressmen boycotted the ceremony. About fifteen thousand dissident young people met at the Lincoln Memorial and the Washington Monument to protest and demonstrate. The city was under the watchful eye of the police and the Army.

Hatless and without a topcoat in forty-degree weather, Richard M. Nixon gave his second inaugural address, from a temporary portico adjacent to the East Front of the Capitol. Facing him seated in temporary seats were 20,000 and thousands more stood in the background. The speech, of course, was carried to the nation via radio and television. The New York *Times* reported that shouts of antiwar demonstrators could be faintly heard, from time to time, coming from a demonstration at the Union Station, three blocks away.

The speech, for the most part written by the President himself, was about seventeen hundred words in length and took about seventeen minutes to deliver. Richard L. Stout (*The Christian Science Monitor,* January 23, 1973) thought that the tone of the speech was "grave and rather stern." James Reston of the New York *Times* (January, 1973) noted that it was "personal and plain" and that it "avoided the excessive rhetoric and promises of the first inaugural address." *The Christian Science Monitor* reported that the listeners responded to the "speech warmly but not enthusiastically and applauded fourteen times" (January 23, 1973).

[1] Address delivered in Washington, D.C., January 20, 1973.

[2] For biographical note, see Appendix.

Among the best and the most quoted presidential inaugural addresses are those of Thomas Jefferson, Abraham Lincoln, Woodrow Wilson, Franklin D. Roosevelt, and John F. Kennedy. From the more recent ones, we frequently quote such sentences as "The only thing we have to fear is fear itself" (Roosevelt, 1933) and "Ask not what your country can do for you—ask what you can do for your country" (Kennedy, 1961). Any President at the beginning of his term hopes to cast poignant thoughts into language that will ring in public consciousness and provide favorite epigrams or distilled thoughts for posterity. But there is indeed truth in Lester Thonssen's conclusion, "By and large distinguished inaugural addresses are scarce. Admittedly it is a difficult speech form." (REPRESENTATIVE AMERICAN SPEECHES: 1960-1961, page 35)

What makes an inaugural address difficult to prepare? First, most obviously, the President labors under the realization that his remarks must stand comparison with those of his predecessors; consequently, he must strive to equal or excel what has come before. Hoping for a polished speech, the President enlists the best talent available for the drafting process. Second, the President knows that his performance during the following four years will be measured by what he says on this occasion. Furthermore, he knows that he has center stage and must not only issue a policy statement but also endeavor to unite the factions and inspire the citizens. Third, the President must attempt to cast what he says in fresh and impressive language. Quite likely he may utter some of the thoughts that his predecessors have mentioned or what he has said during the campaign, or even during a first term. But he must respect time restrictions imposed by the nature of the occasion and broadcast limitations.

Mr. Vice President, Mr. Speaker, Mr. Chief Justice, Senator Cook, Mrs. Eisenhower, and my fellow citizens of this great and good country we share together.

When we met here four years ago, America was bleak in spirit, depressed by the prospect of seemingly endless war abroad and of destructive conflict at home.

As we meet here today, we stand on the threshold of a new era of peace in the world.

The central question before us is: How shall we use that peace?

Let us resolve that this era we are about to enter will not be what other post-war periods have so often been: a time of retreat and isolation that leads to stagnation at home and invites new danger abroad.

Let us resolve that this will be what it can become: a time of great responsibilities greatly borne, in which we renew the spirit and the promise of America as we enter our third century as a Nation.

This past year saw far-reaching results from our new policies for peace. By continuing to revitalize our traditional friendships, and by our missions to Peking and to Moscow, we were able to establish the base for a new and more durable pattern of relationships among the nations of the world. Because of America's bold initiatives, 1972 will be long remembered as the year of the greatest progress since the end of World War II toward a lasting peace in the world.

The peace we seek in the world is not the flimsy peace which is merely an interlude between wars, but a peace which can endure for generations to come.

It is important that we understand both the necessity and the limitations of America's role in maintaining that peace.

Unless we in America work to preserve the peace, there will be no peace.

Unless we in America work to preserve freedom, there will be no freedom.

But let us clearly understand the new nature of America's role, as a result of the new policies we have adopted over these past four years.

We shall respect our treaty commitments.

We shall support vigorously the principle that no country has the right to impose its will or rule on another by force.

We shall continue, in this era of negotiation, to work for the limitation of nuclear arms, and to reduce the danger of confrontation between the great powers.

We shall do our share in defending peace and freedom in the world. But we shall expect others to do their share.

The time has passed when America will make every other nation's conflict our own, or make every other nation's future our responsibility, or presume to tell the people of other nations how to manage their own affairs.

Just as we respect the right of each nation to determine its own future, we also recognize the responsibility of each nation to secure its own future.

Just as America's role is indispensable in preserving the world's peace, so is each nation's role indispensable in preserving its own peace.

Together with the rest of the world, let us resolve to move forward from the beginnings we have made. Let us continue to bring down the walls of hostility which have divided the world for too long, and to build in their place bridges of understanding—so that despite profound differences between systems of government, the people of the world can be friends.

Let us build a structure of peace in the world in which the weak are as safe as the strong—in which each respects the right of the other to live by a different system—in which those who would influence others will do so by the strength of their ideas and not by the force of their arms.

Let us accept that high responsibility not as a burden, but gladly—gladly because the chance to build such a peace is the noblest endeavor in which a nation can engage; gladly also because only if we act greatly in meeting our responsibilities abroad will we remain a great Nation, and only if we remain a great Nation will we act greatly in meeting our challenges at home.

We have the chance today to do more than ever before in our history, to make life better in America—to ensure better education, better health, better housing, better transportation, a cleaner environment—to restore respect for law, to make our communities more livable—and to ensure the God-given right of every American to full and equal opportunity.

Because the range of our needs is so great—because the reach of our opportunities is so great—let us be bold in our determination to meet those needs in new ways.

Just as building a structure of peace abroad has required turning away from old policies that have failed, so building a new era of progress at home requires turning away from old policies that have failed.

Abroad, the shift from old policies to new has not been a retreat from our responsibilities, but a better way to peace.

And at home, the shift from old policies to new will not be a retreat from our responsibilities, but a better way to progress.

Abroad and at home, the key to those new responsibilities lies in the placing and the division of responsibility. We have lived too long with the consequences of attempting to gather all power and responsibility in Washington.

Abroad and at home, the time has come to turn away from the condescending policies of paternalism—of "Washington knows best."

A person can be expected to act responsibly only if he has responsibility. This is human nature. So let us encourage individuals at home and nations abroad to do more for themselves, to decide more for themselves. Let us locate responsibility in more places. And let us measure what we will do for others by what they will do for themselves.

That is why today I offer no promises of a purely governmental solution for every problem. We have lived too long with that false promise. In trusting too much in government, we have asked of it more than it can deliver. This leads only to inflated expectations, to reduced individual effort, and to a disappointment and frustration that erode confidence both in what government can do and in what people can do.

Government must learn to take less from people so that people can do more for themselves.

Let us remember that America was built not by government, but by people—not by welfare, but by work—not by shirking responsibility, but by seeking responsibility.

In our own lives, let each of us ask—not just what will government do for me, but what can I do for myself?

In the challenges we face together, let each of us ask—not just how can government help, but how can I help?

Your national government has a great and vital role to play. And I pledge to you that where this government should act, we will act boldly and we will lead boldly. But just as important is the role that each and every one of us must play, as an individual and as a member of his own community.

From this day forward, let each of us make a solemn commitment in his own heart: to bear his responsibility, to do his part, to live his ideals—so that together, we can see the dawn of a new age of progress for America, and together, as we celebrate our two hundreth anniversary as a nation, we can do so proud in the fulfillment of our promise to ourselves and to the world.

As America's longest and most difficult war comes to an end, let us again learn to debate our differences with civility and decency. And let each of us reach out for that one precious quality government cannot provide—a new level of respect for the rights and feelings of one another, a new level of respect for the individual human dignity which is the cherished birthright of every American.

Above all else, the time has come for us to renew our faith in ourselves and in America.

In recent years, that faith has been challenged.

Our children have been taught to be ashamed of their country, ashamed of their parents, ashamed of America's record at home and its role in the world.

At every turn we have been beset by those who find everything wrong with America and little that is right. But I am confident that this will not be the judgment of history on these remarkable times in which we are privileged to live.

America's record in this century has been unparalleled in the world's history for its responsibility, for its generosity, for its creativity and for its progress.

Let us be proud that our system has produced and provided more freedom and more abundance, more widely shared, than any system in the history of the world.

Let us be proud that in each of the four wars in which we have been engaged in this century, including the one we are now bringing to an end, we have fought not for our selfish advantage, but to help others resist aggression.

And let us be proud that by our bold, new initiatives, by our steadfastness for peace with honor, we have made a breakthrough toward creating in the world what the world has not known before—a structure of peace that can last, not merely for our time, but for generations to come.

We are embarking here today on an era that presents challenges as great as those any nation or any generation has ever faced.

We shall answer to God, to history, and to our conscience for the way in which we use these years.

As I stand in this place, so hallowed by history, I think of others who have stood here before me. I think of the dreams they had for America and I think of how each recognized that he needed help far beyond himself in order to make those dreams come true.

Today I ask your prayer that in the years ahead I may have God's help in making decisions that are right for America and I pray for your help so that together we may be worthy of our challenge.

Let us pledge together to make these next four years the best four years in America's history, so that on its two hundredth birthday America will be as young and as vital as when it began, and as bright a beacon of hope for all the world.

Let us go forward from here confident in hope, strong in our faith in one another, sustained by our faith in God who created us, and striving always to serve His purpose.

AMERICAN POLITICS: A PERSONAL VIEW [3]

GEORGE S. MCGOVERN [4]

To the surprise of many observers George McGovern won the Democratic nomination for the presidency. He arrived at the Democratic convention in early July with enough pledged votes to control the convention. Edwin D. Canham of *The Christian Science Monitor* observed that the Democratic party was "trying to find itself," that emerging "new forces" were "yeasty, uncontrolled, undisciplined, zealous" and that the young, the black, the poor, the women were there "in a trial of new-found strength." But McGovern was unable to enlist the enthusiasm of conservative Democrats and large segments of the labor vote. A hard-hitting campaign (see Preface) was not enough to defeat the incumbent Richard Nixon. After twenty-two months of stumping, the South Dakota senator carried only Massachusetts and the District of Columbia. He suffered the worst defeat in American history. In his concession speech he said: "We will shed no tears because all of this effort I am positive will bear fruit for years to come."

Following his defeat, George McGovern waited until January 21, 1973, to deliver a major speech. In late January he traveled to England, probably to avoid the pain of witnessing the elaborate inaugural celebration of President Nixon. In a London hotel, he watched the President take the oath of office on television. The following day, Sunday, January 21, 1973, the South Dakota senator spoke to the United Nations Youth and Student Association at the Oxford Union (*The Times,* London, January 22, 1973).

The speech stirred some criticism in this country. The Washington *Post* called it an "unfortunate and rather embarrassing speech," objecting to what it thought was "the petulant self-pitying tone and the inaccurate and misleading conclusions that flowed from it." Senator Barry Goldwater of Arizona, who had tasted defeat in 1964, criticized Senator McGovern for not accepting "his defeat in good grace." Senator Goldwater went on to say:

> Mr. President, I perhaps have a better idea than most of how a man feels following a resounding defeat

[3] Speech delivered at Oxford Union, Oxford University, England, January 21, 1973. Quoted by permission.

[4] For biographical note, see Appendix.

> for national office, so I feel qualified to offer Senator McGovern a word of advice. That advice is that the American people appreciate a good loser, but they have absolutely no sympathy with a sorehead. If anyone's behavior can be said to be peculiar at this time, when peace negotiations in Paris are at their most delicate stage, it is the behavior of the Democrat Senator from South Dakota.

In light of subsequent developments many persons will no doubt agree with Senator James Abourezk's (Democrat, South Dakota) opposite view:

> The address was a thoughtful study of an issue which has preoccupied most of us since the first days of the session—the concentration of power in the White House, in defiance of the spirit of the Constitution and in denial of the interests of the Congress, the free press, and the American people.

McGovern, the only senator with a Ph.D. degree, is an effective and earnest speaker, but he is not particularly eloquent. One observer termed his speeches "adequate, rather than eloquent." (Richard Stout, *The Christian Science Monitor,* July 22, 1972) He has been described as "handsome, open-faced, smiling, usually understanding, generally cool, smartly dressed, outwardly confident." (Edwin D. Canham, *The Christian Science Monitor,* June 7, 1972)

I had hoped to be occupied elsewhere today. But the American electorate has made it possible for me to spend this time with you.

Had my fellow citizens been better acquainted with your history, they might have seen certain parallels between Richard Nixon and his namesakes who sat on the English throne.

Like Richard I, Richard Nixon has been celebrated for his foreign journeys, while his own land has been troubled and unattended.

Like Richard II, who wasted England's wealth in a failing war in Ireland, Richard Nixon has squandered America's good name in a foolish venture in Indochina.

And like Richard III, if we can believe the Tudor historians, Richard Nixon has usurped powers that are not his in law or tradition.

You have been spared a King Richard IV. We seem to have him—for four more years.

Only the voters of Massachusetts—the nation's birthplace—and of Washington, D.C.—the nation's capital—would have had it otherwise. We have established a new political dictum: "As Massachusetts goes, so goes the District of Columbia."

Just why the American electorate gave the present Administration such an overwhelming mandate in November remains something of a mystery to me. I do not expect to find a fully satisfactory answer. We worked so incredibly hard and campaigned so fairly and openly, that our overwhelming defeat has left us with a temporary sense of sadness and fury that we must learn to direct into a constructive, continuing effort to restore the best hopes of America. I firmly believed throughout 1971 that the major hurdle to winning the Presidency was winning the Democratic nomination. I believed that any reasonable Democrat could defeat President Nixon. I now think that no one could have defeated him in 1972. And I am not certain that the Democratic Congress will hold him in check for the next four years. I am convinced that the United States is closer to one-man rule than at any time in our history—and this paradoxically by a President who is not popular.

Fundamentally, we have experienced an exhaustion of important institutions in America. Today only the Presidency is activist and strong, while other traditional centers of power are timid and depleted. This is why one man in the White House was able for so long to continue a conflict of madness in Southeast Asia hated by so many of his countrymen.

The institution of Congress has been exhausted by executive encroachment and legislative paralysis. For a decade, a war was waged without congressional approval; for years, that war raged on in part due to congressional inaction. The representatives of the people proved unwilling to end a policy opposed by the people.

But the impotence of Congress and the omnipotence of the Presidency have deeper roots and a longer history. In 1933, the Senate and the House passed Administration bills almost before they were printed or read. It was a time of crisis. But in the years since then, the Congress has acted as though the crisis were permanent. We now accept the curious notion that the legislative initiative rests with the executive branch. Indeed, students of American government are themselves surprised at the startling fact that nearly 90 percent of the legislation the Congress considers originates with the Administration.

And in the last generation, presidential activism and congressional passivity have been even more pronounced in the field of foreign policy. Congress was not asked for approval in the 1950s before American troops were dispatched to Korea and Lebanon. The chairman of the Senate Foreign Relations Committee, who advised against the Bay of Pigs invasion, was ignored, while other members of Congress were not even consulted. The Senate was assured that the Gulf of Tonkin Resolution was no writ for a wider war; it was then used as an excuse for the widest war since 1945.

Now this tide—which has ebbed and flowed for four decades—has crested at a new high. Just before Christmas, the President, in the flush of his electoral landslide, unleashed the most barbarous bombing of the war without even forewarning the Congress. He then refused to explain it or to permit any of his subordinates to explain it—a situation which must strike you especially as strange, since not only the Foreign Secretary but the Prime Minister are regularly called to account in the House of Commons.

I only wish your government had expressed to us the moral outrage that a good friend was obligated to express against the Nixon destruction of Indochina. Thank God for the eloquent and timely words of Roy Jenkins.

The President's defense for silence over this arbitrary bombardment and secret negotiations was the American doctrine of executive privilege, which is supposed to protect certain limited types of communication within the executive branch. The truth is that he was abusing executive privilege, which is not supposed to prevent review and the exercise of responsibility by the legislative branch.

Our Constitution, like yours, is an organic document. Although the first Americans sketched the essential outlines of government, they wisely left the embellishment of the relationship among its three branches to experience. Thus, the assignment of specific authority is only in a few instances explicit.

But among the rights clearly assigned to the Congress are the powers of war and peace and the power of the purse. The power to make or unmake war, however, has been stripped almost completely from the Senate and the House. And now, for the first time, the executive has mounted a serious challenge to the congressional control of appropriations. Perhaps the Congress invited this attack by a complacent acquiescence in the Vietnam disaster; in any case, the battle is on, and the Congress is losing.

Last fall, we submitted to the President a bill to clean up our nation's waterways. He vetoed the bill, and we passed it again over his veto. He then simply refused to spend the money as Congress directed. The success of this tactic was followed by the impoundment of funds for other domestic programs. Most incredibly, at the end of the last legislative session the President demanded that the Congress rubber stamp such impoundments in advance. He asked us to agree to set a budgetary ceiling within which the sole power of appropriation was reserved to the executive branch. Even more incredible was the speed with which the House of Representatives approved this request, and its relatively narrow defeat in the Senate. And after Congress refused the President this authority, he just took it. One wonders why he even bothered to ask.

This is not the way of a government of laws or even of men, but of one man. Today the United States is moving dangerously in that direction. The Congress seems incapable of stopping what it opposes or securing what it seeks. It has been described by a Republican senator as a "third- or fourth-rate power" in Washington. And it may be fairly asked whether the Congress of the United States in the seventh decade of this century is in peril of going the way of the House of Lords in the first decade. The difference is that the diminution of the Lords made English government more democratic, while the diminution of the Congress makes American government more dictatorial.

And the exhaustion of the Congress is matched by the exhaustion of the political parties.

The Republican Party, reduced to utter vassalage by the White House, offers little more than administrative reorganization. They offer the politics of efficiency—but to what end and impact? Their answer to the transportation crisis is to rearrange the Department of Transportation. Their answer to desperate social needs is to reduce and rename social programs. Their answer to the threat of racism is the malignancy of benign neglect. Their answer to the housing crisis is a moratorium on new public housing.

And at the same time, the loyal opposition is neither loyal to a specific set of ideas nor effective in its opposition. The Democratic Party is in peril of becoming a party of incumbency out of power, much like the Whigs of the nineteenth century—a party with no principles, no programs, living only from day to day, caring only for the perquisites of office, doing nothing, and worse, not caring that nothing is done.

Though important and, I believe, enduring reforms have opened the Democratic Party to broader citizen participation, the purposes for which it stands remain disputed and undefined. For twenty-eight of the last forty years, those purposes were set by Democratic Presidents in the White House. Today, the party consists largely of fragments and factions, often still divided along the same lines as in 1968, when pro-Administration and anti-war forces contended for its soul.

At the same time, the Democratic constituency has declined; in both of the last national elections, the Democratic candidate could count only 40 percent of the vote. I believe the party is still the best hope and help of the unprivileged majority of Americans. Yet I know that we have failed to convey the Democratic appeal to millions who are not racist, but afraid; who do not seek a Wallace, but will settle for him if no one else seems to hear or heed them.

And what is the response of the Democratic Party and its major ally in organized labor? Not a determined effort to shape a constituency for change, but an exhausted armistice with the status quo. In 1973, the party itself is no longer a challenging source of ideas and innovation in society. Indeed, in the midst of the quarrels and the contention, the safest course for party officials has been to emphasize that they are interested, not in the ideology, but in the technology of politics.

Without principles, there is no party. And a nation cannot be led nobly or even decently by a collection of politicians whose highest purpose is power.

But perhaps the most discouraging development of recent years is the exhaustion of the institution of the press.

Under constant pressure from an administration that appears to believe that the right of a free press is the right to print or say what they agree with, the media have yielded subtly but substantially. During the campaign, I was subjected to the close, critical reporting that is a tradition in American politics. It was not always comfortable, but it is always necessary. Yet Mr. Nixon escaped a similar scrutiny. The press never really laid a glove on him, and they seldom told the people that he was hiding or that his plans for the next four years were hidden. Six days after the Watergate gang was run to the ground, Mr. Nixon invited reporters into his office, and submitted to the only interrogation his managers allowed during the fall campaign. Not a single reporter could gather the courage to ask a question about the bugging and burglary of the Democratic National Committee. Much of this can be blamed on the incestuous character of the White House press corps itself. Ask one wrong question, and a reporter may find himself cut off altogether, thus ending his repose in one of the cushiest assignments a journalist can draw.

Now, with the election over, the executive branch has tightened the pressure on the media. For example, the Administration has expressed an intention to punish offending television networks by depriving their stations of licenses. Already, the White House has dismantled the Public Broadcasting System whose public affairs presentations the President found irritating. And the press has responded by retreating. It has catalogued the slashes in domestic programs and the plans for arbitrary, insensitive government—but it has not even noticed anything amiss in the fact that these steps were concealed or denied before the election. There are, of course, brave reporters, newspapers, and television channels ready to take the heat; but there are countless others who have left the kitchen for a more comfortable, uncritical existence in the antechamber of this Administration. They are trying to get along by going along. The more wrong-headed and irresponsible are far more interested in cultivating their dubious "sources" on the inside than they are in presenting accurate information or thoughtful judgements. Fortunately, their reading audience is small and increasingly wary of ill-informed gossip.

And the exhaustion of American institutions is matched by an exhaustion of the American spirit.

This even touches some liberal intellectuals, traditionally the most tireless group in America. Today you can hear such liberals saying that government cannot make any real difference for good in the lives of people—that whatever it touches will turn to failure. Many of those who supported the advances of the 1960s so fervently now denounce with equal fervor the setbacks of the 1960s. And they are reluctant to resume the imperfect but important march interrupted by the war. Instead they seem almost happy to fulfill the prophecy of W. R. Inge, the Gloomy Dean, that he who would marry the spirit of the age soon finds himself a widower. And they seem to draw a curious personal consolation from the evidence that my appeals to the idealism and morality of America were rejected by the majority of Americans.

Indeed, these so-called liberals now tell us that we should not try to save our cities, cure the causes of crime, eradicate poverty or admit our error in Vietnam. They say that if we are part of the solution, then we are also part of the problem. Their motto appears to be: "Nothing ventured, nothing lost." They seem to be searching for the lowest common denominator of the current political mood.

The same dispirit envelops millions of other Americans. They have followed a bloody trail of disappointment from a sunny street in Dallas to a hotel kitchen in Los Angeles. Three times they have voted for peace; and each time they have been given more war. They were oversold on the social experiments of the 1960s; now they are wary of buying even sensible and essential social progress from any political leader. They see government as at best an annoyance, at worst an enemy, and they wish it would just leave them alone. Broken promises have ended in broken power. Public officials are viewed principally as annoying tax collectors.

To my mind, this mood was central to the outcome of the 1972 election. For example, the commentators have suggested that credibility was among my principal difficulties during the campaign. I agree, but not with the proposition that people did not believe me. I think they *did* believe that I would do what I said, and they were afraid. Many Americans looked back at the debris of the last decade, and they feared that once again, they were about to face a hard effort and harvest nothing from it.

ministration's consent for the appropriate officials
efore House and Senate committees.

e used to stop executive wars by whim. The Con-
refuse to fund conflicts it has not declared or
ed to fight. From the tragedy and travail of Viet-
Congress at least must learn the truth of Edmund
rning: "The thing you fight for is not the thing
recover; but depreciated, sunk, wasted and con-
the contest." American ideals have been depreci-
rican wealth has been sunk. Human lives have
d, and Indochina itself has been consumed in the
he United States must fight when the course is
never again should the Congress allow young
lives to be lost for the defense of a corrupt dic-
here in the world.

ese steps are only a beginning. For if the Congress
e a role of leadership, it must have not only the
ower to review and reverse policy, but also the
wer to make policy in the first place. It must
gh—so it will not hear the reply that the Presi-
s knows best. It must be structured for integrated
aking—so it will not hear the reply that only the
an pull all the pieces together.

e Congress should establish a unified budget as-
echanism. The Senate and House should estab-
mittee to estimate revenues, set a general level
tures, and establish priorities to relate specific
on decisions to that general level. This com-
ld have sufficient resources of expertise and in-
There is no reason to let the President control
because he has the only Office of Management
.

the Congress should establish a similar mecha-
tional security policy. With members drawn from
riations, Foreign Relations and Armed Services
, such a unified committee could offer a thought-

So to me the central challenge for the future of American politics is to end the paralysis of institutions and ease the apprehensions of the electorate. The United States must find a way to replace exhaustion with energy, cynicism with hope, resignation with determination, destructive anger with constructive activism.

That is so easy to say, so hard to do.

I no longer think it can be done merely by calls to greatness or appeals to idealism, no matter how eloquent. Americans have been told until they are tired of hearing it that they shall overcome, that they can move their country forward, that they can have a great society, that they can seek a newer world or find the lift of a driving dream—or even bring America home to its founding ideals. This kind of summons has value; indeed, in my view, Americans are desperately anxious to believe in a transcendent, almost mystical purpose. But they are also skeptical now of any such summons unless there are signs of progress already there.

As I discovered in the last campaign, it is not even enough to outline proposals in specific detail. The only way to reawaken faith in the system is for government and politicians to restore it step by step, through substantive advances that mean something to people. They must see their sons home from Vietnam, their neighborhood crime rate reduced, their taxes used to build better lives instead of bigger bureaucracies, their children educated in decent schools and their illnesses cared for at reasonable cost. The progress must be visible, sure and steady. The words of politicians must be matched by effort.

This requires above all else a determined effort to improve and strengthen the institutions in America that are supposed to serve the citizens of America. After a decade of disillusion, institutions may be unfashionable things. But institutions are not evil, they are neutral; and they are indispensable instruments of change in society. More often than not, the ebbs and tides of history are determined by the nuts and bolts of government.

In modern times, when American liberals have recognized that truth, they have tended to see it in terms of the Presidency. Only a few years ago, liberal scholarship still celebrated the strong executive and sought to strengthen it even more. Now we have learned that the Presidency, too, is a neutral instrument—that power in the White House can be abused as well as used—that a reactionary or a warmaker can also read Richard Neustadt and James MacGregor Burns.

Twice now our answer has been an attempt to change the person in the Presidency. Both times we have ended in at least as much difficulty as we were before. It is now almost four years until the next national election. It is also time to ask whether American progressives should continue to rely on a quadrennial chance to capture what is becoming an elective dictatorship.

We may lose again as we have before. And liberty is the real loser when so much authority is vested in a single office.

There will be plenty of time to prepare for the next campaign. But now is the time for a determined effort to change, not the person in the White House, but the power of the Presidency. American liberals must reverse the forty-year trend toward a stronger President and return to the two-hundred-year-old tradition of shared power. It is time to renew the Constitution, the Bill of Rights and the Declaration of Independence.

The Supreme Court is subject to fate and executive appointment, with only the Senate standing between the court and an ideological coup. So the true priority is to protect the place of the Congress in the federal system. We must seek a pluralism of power, where Congress and the President guard and prod each other. And there must be a new devotion to personal liberty and personal privacy in America.

Some political scientists claim that this is the wrong aim. They say: Only the President can lead because only the President has a mandate. But Congress has a collective mandate, made by a blend and balance of the regional interests reflected

in each member's election.
be as effective as the Presid
gress can work to check the
try. It can seek cooperatio
shape a kind of cooperativ
change happen. In the w
"That which is in oppositi
that differ comes . . . harmo

In pursuit of a plural
powerful weapons at its di
ocation without peer or pr
long last seems ready to act.

Now the Congress mus
full measure of influence.
tion that allows the Presi
comes up for renewal, the
issue another blank check.
assure that profits, divide
again permitted a special
bear the full burden.

But the Congress shoul
It should mount a consist
on its foremost power—co
Madison wrote in *The Fe*

> The power over the purse
> complete and effectual weap
> arm the immediate represent
> redress of every grievance, and
> salutary measure.

This insight is borne ou
For five centuries, from E
liberty was purchased piec
power of the purse. And i
of the purse can sustain Am

It can be used to stop
Part or perhaps all of an ap

on the A
to testify

It can
gress mu
even deci
nam, the
Burke's
which yo
sumed in
ated. An
been was
contest.
right. B
America
tator any

And
is to ass
negative
positive
know er
dent alw
decision
Presider

First
sessmen
lish a c
of expe
appropr
mittee s
formati
the buc
and Bu

Seco
nism fo
the Ap
Commi

So to me the central challenge for the future of American politics is to end the paralysis of institutions and ease the apprehensions of the electorate. The United States must find a way to replace exhaustion with energy, cynicism with hope, resignation with determination, destructive anger with constructive activism.

That is so easy to say, so hard to do.

I no longer think it can be done merely by calls to greatness or appeals to idealism, no matter how eloquent. Americans have been told until they are tired of hearing it that they shall overcome, that they can move their country forward, that they can have a great society, that they can seek a newer world or find the lift of a driving dream—or even bring America home to its founding ideals. This kind of summons has value; indeed, in my view, Americans are desperately anxious to believe in a transcendent, almost mystical purpose. But they are also skeptical now of any such summons unless there are signs of progress already there.

As I discovered in the last campaign, it is not even enough to outline proposals in specific detail. The only way to reawaken faith in the system is for government and politicians to restore it step by step, through substantive advances that mean something to people. They must see their sons home from Vietnam, their neighborhood crime rate reduced, their taxes used to build better lives instead of bigger bureaucracies, their children educated in decent schools and their illnesses cared for at reasonable cost. The progress must be visible, sure and steady. The words of politicians must be matched by effort.

This requires above all else a determined effort to improve and strengthen the institutions in America that are supposed to serve the citizens of America. After a decade of disillusion, institutions may be unfashionable things. But institutions are not evil, they are neutral; and they are indispensable instruments of change in society. More often than not, the ebbs and tides of history are determined by the nuts and bolts of government.

In modern times, when American liberals have recognized that truth, they have tended to see it in terms of the Presidency. Only a few years ago, liberal scholarship still celebrated the strong executive and sought to strengthen it even more. Now we have learned that the Presidency, too, is a neutral instrument—that power in the White House can be abused as well as used—that a reactionary or a warmaker can also read Richard Neustadt and James MacGregor Burns.

Twice now our answer has been an attempt to change the person in the Presidency. Both times we have ended in at least as much difficulty as we were before. It is now almost four years until the next national election. It is also time to ask whether American progressives should continue to rely on a quadrennial chance to capture what is becoming an elective dictatorship.

We may lose again as we have before. And liberty is the real loser when so much authority is vested in a single office.

There will be plenty of time to prepare for the next campaign. But now is the time for a determined effort to change, not the person in the White House, but the power of the Presidency. American liberals must reverse the forty-year trend toward a stronger President and return to the two-hundred-year-old tradition of shared power. It is time to renew the Constitution, the Bill of Rights and the Declaration of Independence.

The Supreme Court is subject to fate and executive appointment, with only the Senate standing between the court and an ideological coup. So the true priority is to protect the place of the Congress in the federal system. We must seek a pluralism of power, where Congress and the President guard and prod each other. And there must be a new devotion to personal liberty and personal privacy in America.

Some political scientists claim that this is the wrong aim. They say: Only the President can lead because only the President has a mandate. But Congress has a collective mandate, made by a blend and balance of the regional interests reflected

in each member's election. And that collective mandate can be as effective as the President's universal mandate. The Congress can work to check the Executive and to move the country. It can seek cooperation with the President; it can also shape a kind of cooperative tension with him that can make change happen. In the words of an ancient philosopher: "That which is in opposition is in concert, and from things that differ comes . . . harmony."

In pursuit of a pluralism of power, the Congress has powerful weapons at its disposal. And after executive provocation without peer or precedent, the legislative branch at long last seems ready to act.

Now the Congress must exert its authority to achieve a full measure of influence. For example, when the legislation that allows the President to control wages and prices comes up for renewal, the Senate and the House should not issue another blank check. We should include safeguards to assure that profits, dividends and interest rates are never again permitted a special break while the wages of workers bear the full burden.

But the Congress should not wait for such opportunities. It should mount a consistent and coherent effort, founded on its foremost power—control over appropriations. James Madison wrote in *The Federalist Papers,* number 58:

> The power over the purse may, in fact, be regarded as the most complete and effectual weapon with which any constitution can arm the immediate representatives of the people, for obtaining a redress of every grievance, and for carrying into effect every just and salutary measure.

This insight is borne out in the history of your own land. For five centuries, from Edward I to George III, English liberty was purchased piece by piece by the Parliamentary power of the purse. And in 1973, the congressional power of the purse can sustain American liberty.

It can be used to stop the abuse of executive privilege. Part or perhaps all of an appropriation could be conditioned

on the Administration's consent for the appropriate officials to testify before House and Senate committees.

It can be used to stop executive wars by whim. The Congress must refuse to fund conflicts it has not declared or even decided to fight. From the tragedy and travail of Vietnam, the Congress at least must learn the truth of Edmund Burke's warning: "The thing you fight for is not the thing which you recover; but depreciated, sunk, wasted and consumed in the contest." American ideals have been depreciated. American wealth has been sunk. Human lives have been wasted, and Indochina itself has been consumed in the contest. The United States must fight when the course is right. But never again should the Congress allow young American lives to be lost for the defense of a corrupt dictator anywhere in the world.

And these steps are only a beginning. For if the Congress is to assume a role of leadership, it must have not only the negative power to review and reverse policy, but also the positive power to make policy in the first place. It must know enough—so it will not hear the reply that the President always knows best. It must be structured for integrated decision making—so it will not hear the reply that only the President can pull all the pieces together.

First, the Congress should establish a unified budget assessment mechanism. The Senate and House should establish a committee to estimate revenues, set a general level of expenditures, and establish priorities to relate specific appropriation decisions to that general level. This committee should have sufficient resources of expertise and information. There is no reason to let the President control the budget because he has the only Office of Management and Budget.

Second, the Congress should establish a similar mechanism for national security policy. With members drawn from the Appropriations, Foreign Relations and Armed Services Committees, such a unified committee could offer a thought-

ful and sensible alternative to executive proposals. This committee, too, should have the necessary resources. If the President can have two State Departments, the Congress can have at least one agency to provide information and recommendations about foreign affairs and defense policy.

Third, the Congress should adjust the seniority system. No other legislative body in the Western world uses length of service as the sole standard for place and power in its committees. If the Congress is to carry out its collective mandate, it must do what the mandate means, not what a few individuals from safe districts want. An activist, effective Congress must reflect the popular will. It cannot do so unless the members freely elect committee chairmen.

Finally, the Congress should defend its powers as it extends them. It must consider and choose from a number of alternatives to cancel or control the impoundment of its appropriations. Only then can the Congress assure the execution of the policies it has enacted.

So if the Congress has the will, there is a way to exercise positive leadership. For the long term, the question is—in what direction?

I am convinced still that the society to which America should aspire is a liberal one. To those who charge that liberalism has been tried and found wanting, I answer that the failure is not in the idea, but in the course of recent history. The New Deal was ended by World War II. The New Frontier was closed by Berlin, Cuba and an imaginary missile gap. And the Great Society lost its greatness in the jungles of Indochina.

Of course, liberal programs will sometimes fail anyway, for human decisions are frail always. Government is the creation of men and encompasses the weaknesses of men. Plans can be poorly executed—though a Congress with sense and a bit of intelligence can work to prevent that. But that government is best, I believe, that best serves the demands of justice. So what Americans should seek is a system in which the principles of civil equality and individual liberty have the highest claim on statesmanship. We must strive to provide a decent standard of life for all citizens and to redistribute wealth and power so each citizen has a fair share. And along with this must come a foreign policy which puts humanity and morality ahead of Cold War myths and the prestige of leaders who would rather compound error than face reality.

And an institutional revival of the Congress not only can lead America in a new direction; it can also spark a similar institutional revival outside government.

Where power is pluralistic rather than presidential, the press will not have so much to fear from the executive branch. It could institute reforms such as the rotation of correspondents at the White House and among candidates in a national election, and the assignment of political reporters and not just "regulars" to the President during a campaign.

There are also hopeful signs of a reawakening in the Democratic Party. The party is scheduled to hold biennial conferences to set national policy, with the first one next year.

And as Democrats look ahead to 1976, they can be encouraged by the enduring gains of 1972. For I believe my campaign set the manner in which future candidates must seek the Democratic nomination—openly, candidly, not with the traditional strategy of saying as little as possible, but with a pledge to seek and speak the truth. I believe we also set a standard for the conduct of future campaigns—which will have to reveal their contributors and represent the people rather than the politicians. And, hopefully, Americans will not again accept wiretapping, Watergates, and the spectacle of a candidate hiding in the White House. Instead, they will expect at least a commitment to correct wrongs rather than committing them. Finally, I believe our campaign set forth the great issues that will dominate the debate of the 1970s, ranging from tax reform to a rational military budget.

And millions of Democrats, whether they are ordinary citizens or senators, are anxious to carry the banner. I have faith that their energy and efforts can end the exhaustion of the electorate, enlist the country in a coalition of conscience as well as self-interest, and expand the 28 million votes the national ticket won in 1972 into a majority that is right as well as new.

In 1972, I was the beneficiary of the most devoted, idealistic campaign workers ever assembled. They provided the energy and the tough-minded attention to issues and political organization that enabled me to win the Democratic presidential nomination against all the odds makers and political prophets. They did not prevail in November; they remain, however, closest to the enduring spirit of the nation that we ought to honor in the year of our bicentennial, 1976. They are the most effective, dynamic political force in American politics today. No one will win either the Democratic presidential nomination in 1976 or the subsequent presidential election as a Democrat without the active support of this superbly motivated, public-spirited force of Americans.

But as I have noted, the next election is four years away. For the immediate future, the key is the Congress. It must take the initiative and provide the inspiration. It must cure the paralysis and procrastination that have earned it the doubt, the disrespect, and the cynicism of the American people. The New York *Times* recently described the President as a leader who "behaves with the aloofness of a Roman emperor." It is useful to remember that no Roman emperor was crowned until the Roman Senate abdicated.

Before most of you were born, the late Henry Luce described this time in history as the American century. Since then, the United States has learned the hard way that you cannot colonize centuries any more than you can colonize countries. But I would still like to believe that my country has something of value to offer to a beleaguered world.

It is not just our wealth and our technology—though that we should share with those who need it.

And it is not the terrible gift of another Guernica in Indochina.

And surely it is not our power to unleash a nuclear reign of terror, to give the earth a last shimmering moment of light before the endless night.

Throughout our history, America's greatest offering—as I said in accepting the Democratic presidential nomination—has been as "a witness to the world for what is noble and just in human affairs." This is what summoned the dock workers of Manchester to support Abraham Lincoln and the cause of liberty during our Civil War. And this is what America must restore. If we fail, other generations who are not free will look back and say that things cannot be any other way.

So in my mind, the challenge of the American future is to revive our institutions and resume our progress at home while we act abroad with "a decent respect for the opinions of mankind."

THE SEVENTIES: PERPLEXITIES AND PROSPECTS

BLACKS AND THE NIXON ADMINISTRATION: THE NEXT FOUR YEARS[1]

VERNON E. JORDAN, JR.[2]

"Blacks and their special problems have gone out of fashion in government, in politics, and in civic concern," observes Peter Goldman of *Newsweek* (February 19, 1973). This reported shift in attitude has stirred grave concern and bitterness among black leaders in this country. At the Civil Rights Symposium, December 11-12, 1972, at the Lyndon Baines Johnson Library at the University of Texas, Julian Bond, Georgia state legislator and popular leader, gave vent to this frustration, saying: "The hopes and beliefs of black people that racial equality of social justice could be achieved through litigation, legislation, negotiation, occasional direct action, and strong alliances with liberal and centrist groups were supplanted by disillusionment, bitterness, and now, open anger."

One of the most articulate spokesmen for minority rights today is Vernon E. Jordan, Jr., executive director of the National Urban League. Taking up where the late Whitney Young, Jr., his predecessor, left off, Jordan works tirelessly to promote his cause. *Newsweek* (February 19, 1973) says that he "pursues his own job like a perpetual political campaign, traveling thousands of miles each month to exchange views with Administration officials, line up support from business leaders and speak to civic groups and local Urban Leagues."

The Nixon Administration budget proposals aroused Jordan to make a fighting speech before a luncheon at the National Press Club, March 16, 1973. In the second paragraph he stated his conviction clearly and forcefully: "Indeed, the proposed budget is the blueprint for the conversion of a national policy of 'benign neglect' into a policy of active hostility to the hopes, dreams and aspirations of black Americans." He left little doubt

[1] Address delivered at the National Press Club, March 16, 1973, Washington, D.C. Quoted by permission.

[2] For biographical note, see Appendix.

that he interpreted the new budget as another sign of the Administration's indifference to black Americans that would result in hardship and misery among the poor. "Life in 1973 may be better for some people but is not better for black Americans," he argued.

Jordan knows how to lend vividness to his words and thus to inject a moving quality into his speeches. He demonstrates his rhetorical vigor in using such phrases as the following: "hacks away at social spending," "a free fire zone doomed to destruction," "the siren song of local infallibility," "the blast of white silence," "the gut issues of today," "like hiring the wolf to guard the sheep," and "spreads a blight across our land." Those interested in reading another speech by Mr. Jordan will find his address "Survival" in REPRESENTATIVE AMERICAN SPEECHES: 1971-1972, pages 49-58.

In his Budget Message to the Congress, the President once again called for "a new American Revolution to return power to the people." But the Message itself, and the provisions of a federal budget that hacks away at social spending with ruthless intensity, can only be seen as the first shots of a counter-revolution designed to destroy the social reforms of the 1960s.

Indeed, the proposed budget is the blueprint for the conversion of a national policy of "benign neglect" into a policy of active hostility to the hopes, dreams and aspirations of black Americans.

I do not believe this policy is intentional, nor do I believe that it is the product of conscious, anti-black, anti-poor reasoning. Rather it is the by-product of a view of society and of the proper role of government that is incompatible with the implementation of the precious rights won by minorities in recent years. The yawning gap between the philosophy of decentralized government marked by a passive domestic role for the federal Administration, and the effects of such a system on poor people and minorities vividly illustrates how honorable intentions can have disastrous results.

I am reminded of the famous lines by T. S. Eliot: "Between the idea and the reality/ Between the motion and the act/ Falls the shadow." Today that shadow falls on black

Americans, minorities, and on the overwhelming numbers of poor people who are white. It is they who are being asked to carry the burdens imposed by the impending massive federal withdrawal from moral and programmatic leadership in the domestic arena. The shadow that falls upon them is deep and its darkness spreads a blight across our land.

The Administration's domestic policy, as revealed in its budget proposals and in a flurry of public statements, encompasses on the one hand, sharp cuts in spending on social services, and on the other, a massive shift in resources and responsibility from Washington to local governments. These are the two prongs of a pincer movement that entraps millions of Americans.

A brief examination of just a few of the federal actions both proposed and already taken, are enough to indicate that urban America is well on the way to becoming a free fire zone doomed to destruction by the very forces it looks to for salvation.

In employment, the Emergency Employment Act will be phased out, ending public service jobs for about 150,000 state and city employees, some 40 percent of whom had been classified as disadvantaged. Job-creation and -training programs already crippled by the refusal to spend appropriated funds, will be cut sharply. A wide variety of federally backed summer and youth employment programs will be dropped, and special programs for high-unemployment areas will be eliminated.

In housing, a freeze has been imposed on federally subsidized housing affecting hundreds of thousands of low-income families and robbing construction workers of jobs.

In education, federal programs to provide compensatory educational services to disadvantaged children, and important vocational education programs will be dismantled, while day care, student loans, special school milk programs and aid to libraries will be eliminated or reduced to a small fraction of their former size.

In health, 23 million aged and handicapped people will have an extra billion dollars torn from them in higher Medicare charges and lessened coverage, while funds for the successful community mental health centers and for new hospitals will be eliminated.

In addition to this listing of horror stories, there are further atrocities—the dismantling of the Office of Economic Opportunity and abolition of its over nine hundred community action programs; the end of the Model Cities program, and the effective end of urban renewal and a host of other federal programs of community development.

A number of arguments have been advanced to justify the far-reaching changes the new American counter-revolution seeks to establish. Taken together, they recall Horace Walpole's comment about the world: that it "is a comedy to those that think, a tragedy to those that feel."

It is said, for example, that the budget cuts are necessary to avoid new taxes and to control inflation. This neatly avoids mention of the imposition of a sharply increased Social Security payroll tax that falls disproportionately on the same low-income families that will be hurt most by social service cutbacks. I accept the need for a ceiling on federal expenditures, but I cannot accept the faulty priorities that raise military expenditures by just under $5 billion while slicing funds for the poor and for the cities. The cost of one Trident Submarine would pay for the public service employment program. The requested increase in funds for the F-15 fighter is about equal to the amounts cut from manpower training funds. Federal disinvestment in human resources reflects an irrational choice of priorities.

Another reason for the cuts is the overly optimistic view that many of the federal programs are no longer needed. The President himself seemed to be making this point in his Human Resources Message when he said: "By almost any measure life is better for Americans in 1973 than ever before in our history, and better than in any other society of the world in this or any earlier age." And the theme was repeated in the Message dealing with cities, which declared that "the hour of crisis has passed."

I cannot agree. I believe, instead, that the hour of crisis is upon us, and is intensified by the federal withdrawal from urban problems. I would hate to have to explain to a poor black family in Bedford-Stuyvesant that's chained to an overcrowded slum apartment because of the housing subsidy freeze that this is really the best of all possible worlds. I would hate to have to explain to a poor black farm worker in Mississippi that the record gross national product means he's living in a golden era. And I would hate to have to explain to an unemployed Vietnam veteran who can no longer enter a federal manpower training program that he is being adequately repaid for his sacrifices.

Life in 1973 may be better for some people, but it is not better for black Americans. We are afflicted with unemployment rates more than double those for white workers. Black teenage unemployment is near 40 percent. Unemployment and under-employment in the ghettos of America is from one third to one half of the work force. The total number of poor people in this country has risen sharply in the past several years. No. This is no Eden in which we live and we cannot complacently agree that there is no longer a need for federal social service programs.

Another justification for ending some programs is arrived at by a method of reasoning I confess I am unable to comprehend. Such programs, it is said, have proved their worth and therefore the government should no longer operate them. Since they are so good, someone else should do them. I can only suppose that the next step will be to tell the Joint Chiefs of Staff that the armed forces have done such a good job that the federal government will stop funding them.

Another argument—a serious one of some substance—is that some programs have not worked and therefore should be abandoned. Such programs fall into two categories—those that appear to neutral observers to have accomplished their goals, and those that clearly have not been as effective as they should have been.

It is inaccurate and unfair to suggest that the community action programs or the Model Cities programs, to take two important examples, have failed. There is every indication that they have brought a new sense of spirit and accomplishment to many hundreds of cities. By fully involving poor people in the decision-making process they have contributed significantly to urban stability and to individual accomplishment. Federal evaluation studies endorse this view. Local political leadership has also insisted that the programs are successful. For years, the agony of the Vietnam war was justified on the grounds that we had made a moral commitment to the people there. Can we now abandon the moral commitment to our own cities and to our own people?

Some federal programs have been clear disappointments. Some of the housing subsidy programs, for example, were sabotaged not by poor people seeking a decent home, but by some speculators in league with some federal employees. Thus, although thousands of families have been sheltered by these programs; although scandal-free housing has been produced by effective nonprofit organizations and although the need for low- and moderate-income housing is pressing, federal housing subsidies have been frozen and appear on their way to an early death. The victims of federal housing failures are being punished doubly—once by ineffective program control, and again by the moratorium on all housing subsidies. Ending all housing programs because some have shown signs of failure makes about as much sense as eliminating the Navy because some new ships have had cost over-runs.

The final justification of the Administration's policies, and the core of the new American counter-revolution, is that federal funds will be transferred to local governments in the form of bloc grants in four major areas—community development, education, manpower and law enforcement. It is proposed that the federal government end its categorical grant programs administered, financed and monitored by federal agencies and that local governments should now decide whether to spend federal monies on job training or on roads, on compensatory education in the ghetto or on a new high school in the suburbs. This has been called "returning power to the people."

To black Americans, who historically had no choice but to look to the federal government to correct the abuses of state and local governments, that is very much like hiring the wolf to guard the sheep. It is axiomatic in American political life, with some exceptions, that the lower the level of government, the lower the level of competence and the higher the margin for discrimination against the poor and the powerless.

The power that has accrued to the central government is due to the failure of localities to be responsive to the needs of all but a handful of their constituents. Black Americans have looked to the federal government to end slavery, to end peonage, to restore our constitutional rights and to secure economic progress in the face of discrimination. Yes, we looked to Washington because we could not look to Jackson, to Baton Rouge or to Montgomery. White people looked to Washington too, for the federal programs that helped many of them survive the Depression, helped them move to suburbia and helped them to prosper economically. Now that Washington has finally embarked on programs that hold out some hope for minorities, we are told instead to look to local governments notorious for their historic insensitivity to the needs and aspirations of blacks and the poor.

Before falling prey to the siren song of local infallibility, the Administration should examine the use local governments are making of general revenue-sharing grants already distributed. News reports from across the country repeat the same dismal story—federal money used to build new city halls, to raise police salaries, and to cut local taxes. All this is taking place at a time when school systems are falling apart, housing is being abandoned, and health needs are unmet. The record does not inspire confidence that lost federal social service programs will be replaced with effective local ones.

General revenue sharing is a fact. It is a reality. Thirty billion dollars is in the pipeline for state and local governments. Rather than throw still more money at local governments at the expense of federal programs with proven track records, the Administration should be developing performance standards and effective compliance mechanisms that assure these local programs will work. Folding—or rather, crumbling—federal social service programs into no-strings-attached special revenue-sharing packages seems to me to be a prescription for disaster.

Black Americans have been assured that anti-discrimination regulations will prevent local abuses. While the Treasury Department's guidelines have been revised and strengthened, we still cannot take heart from such assurances. They come just a few weeks after the Civil Rights Commission reported the persistence of "inertia of agencies in the field of civil rights," and after the government was subjected to a federal court order to enforce the laws against school segregation. It is hard to imagine that the politically charged decision to withhold funds from states or cities that discriminate will be made. And without federal standards assuring that funds will be used in behalf of poor people in need of job training, public housing, and special school and health programs, the money will once again find its way into the pockets of entrenched local interests.

The proposed special revenue-sharing approach breaks faith not only with poor people, but with local governments as well. What Washington gives with one hand it takes with the other. Mayors who once hungered for no-strings-attached bloc grants are now panicked by the realization that the funds they receive will be inadequate to meet the needs of their communities and will be less than their cities get in the current categorical-aid programs. In addition, there is the probability that future special revenue-sharing funds will continue to shrink. Rather than shifting power to the people, the new American counter-revolution creates a vacuum in responsible power.

We must not forget, as so many have, that federal programs today do embody local initiatives and local decision making. The myth of the Washington bureaucrat making decisions for people three thousand miles away is false. The money often comes from the federal Treasury. The broad program goals and definitions of national needs come, as they should, from the Congress. But the specific program proposals, their implementation, and their support come from local governments, citizens and agencies. Those federal dollars that are now deemed tainted actually enable local citizens to meet local problems under the umbrella of national financial and moral leadership. To shift the center of gravity away from national leadership is to compound the drift and inertia that appear to categorize our society today.

It is in this context that the blast of white silence is so puzzling. Far more white people than blacks will be hurt by the budget cuts. Yet the responsibility for calling attention to their impact falls increasingly on black leadership. There are three times as many poor white families as there are poor black families. The majority of people on welfare are white. Of the black poor, more than half don't get one devalued dollar from welfare. Two thirds of the families who got homes through the now-frozen 235 subsidy program were white. The majority of trainees in manpower programs, and three fourths of the people who will lose their jobs under the public employment program are white.

But because black Americans have been the most vocal segment of the population in urging social reforms, there is the mistaken impression that only blacks benefit from them. The Battle of the Budget is a larger-scale replay of the fight for welfare reform waged—and lost—last year. Then, as now, black leadership was out front in favor of a living guaranteed income for all. But we had few white supporters, although many more white people than black would have benefited. It is reasonable to ask, had we won that struggle would all of those poor white people have returned their income supplement checks? And it is fair to ask today that white people join us in the struggle to preserve the social services of the federal government that enable them, too, to survive.

The silent white majority that has been the prime beneficiary of the programs of the 1960s and is today the group most in need of further federal services will have to speak up. They are not stigmatized, as are blacks, by charges of special pleading by special Americans looking for special treatment. And their representatives in the Congress will have to act, too. They cannot complacently watch their constituents' welfare being trampled on, nor can they accept the shrinkage of their rightful constitutional role in our system of government.

Already, there have been signs that some Congressmen whose votes helped to pass progressive legislation a few short years ago are now of a mind to compromise with Administration power, to compromise the jobs and livelihood and needs of their constituents, to compromise the power of the Congress to control the purse and to influence domestic policies, and finally, to compromise their own principles. If this is so, it will be tragic for the Constitution, tragic for the country, tragic for the poor people, and tragic for the heritage of liberalism.

The gut issues of today—better schools, jobs and housing for all, personal safety and decent health care—are issues that transcend race. So long as they are falsely perceived as "black issues," nothing constructive will be done to deal with them. White America must come to see that *its* cities, *its* needs and *its* economic and physical health are at stake. The needs of blacks and whites are too strongly intwined to separate. As Whitney Young used to say, "We may have come here on different ships, but we're in the same boat now."

So white Americans must join with black people to rekindle the American Dream, and to sing, in the words of Langston Hughes:

> O, let America be America again—
> The land that never has been yet—
> and yet must be.

THE WATERGATE CASE [3]

RICHARD M. NIXON [4]

Probably the most dramatic speech of the year and the most difficult presidential address for Richard M. Nixon was the one that he delivered over radio and television on the night of April 30, 1973. After ten months of minimizing the Watergate incident, the President decided that he could no longer remain silent. Day by day, the charges of misdeeds at the White House and involvement of the FBI and the Department of Justice mounted. The investigations of the Grand Jury and the Senate committee headed by Democratic Senator Sam J. Ervin, Jr., of North Carolina were uncovering embarrassing evidence. Confessions, resignations, firings, and indictments demanded that the President explain to the nation and attempt to restore faith in the presidency.

The episode dated back to June 17, 1972, when five men in the employ of the Committee for the Reelection of the President were apprehended at 2 A.M. bugging the sixth-floor offices of the Democratic National Committee in the plush Watergate complex in Washington. On September 26, Attorney General Kleindienst, who later resigned, said, "I can say categorically that no one of responsibility in the White House or the Campaign Committee had any knowledge [of the bugging]." The arrests, confessions, and convictions of those caught in the break-in and the implication of several White House aides of the President added fuel to the fire. Throughout the fall, while the campaign was in full swing, there continued to be repeated denials of involvement and of attempts to cover up the affair.

The confessions and conviction of the original conspirators did not solve the problem for the Administration. Judge John Sirica, who presided over the trial, thought that the investigation had failed to uncover all the facts; consequently he urged further investigation.

A Senate investigative committee was stymied because the President stopped his aides from divulging information on the Watergate break-in by declaring executive privilege. But other irregularities appeared. The public was disturbed by the reported

[3] Speech delivered by radio and television from the White House, April 30, 1973.

[4] For biographical note, see Appendix.

failure of the National Republican Committee to report certain cash contributions; the revelation of the burglarizing, on orders from a White House aide, of the office of the psychiatrist of Daniel Ellsberg, one of the defendants in the Pentagon Papers case; and the reported destruction of incriminating evidence in the Watergate affair by the acting director of the FBI.

The speech, somewhat like Nixon's Checkers speech delivered in 1952, is not a great speech. Nevertheless, it is important because it reveals much about the sorry nature of the political climate as well as the low standards of morality. Many persons lauded the President for his acceptance of the responsibility for the affair and his assurance that a full investigation would be held. A statement by James Reston of the New York *Times* is representative of the criticism leveled at the speech: "The President's speech was full of self-pity and unconvincing alibis, but as usual it is wiser to pay attention to what he does rather than what he says, and he has done enough to make a new beginning and turn the cover-up into an objective investigation."

In his delivery the President revealed his strain and worry. Tense and haggard, he was not as fluent as usual. In fact, in his introduction he fumbled for words. Throughout the twenty-four minutes of the speech he had some difficulty following his manuscript. Unlike many of his other formal addresses, this speech gave the impression of complete seriousness and eagerness to communicate. The speech was reported to have been of his own composition.

I want to talk to you tonight from my heart on a subject of deep concern to every American.

In recent months, members of my Administration and officials of the Committee for the Reelection of the President—including some of my closest friends and most trusted aides—have been charged with involvement in what has come to be known as the Watergate affair. These include charges of illegal activity during and preceding the 1972 presidential election and charges that responsible officials participated in efforts to cover up that illegal activity.

The inevitable result of these charges has been to raise serious questions about the integrity of the White House itself. Tonight I wish to address those questions.

Last June 17, while I was in Florida trying to get a few days' rest after my visit to Moscow, I first learned from news reports of the Watergate break-in. I was appalled at this senseless, illegal action, and I was shocked to learn that employees of the Reelection Committee were apparently among those guilty. I immediately ordered an investigation by appropriate government authorities. On September 15, as you will recall, indictments were brought against seven defendants in the case.

As the investigations went forward, I repeatedly asked those conducting the investigation whether there was any reason to believe that members of my Administration were in any way involved. I received repeated assurances that there were not. Because of these continuing reassurances—because I believed the reports I was getting, because I had faith in the persons from whom I was getting them—I discounted the stories in the press that appeared to implicate members of my Administration or other officials of the Campaign Committee.

Until March of this year, I remained convinced that the denials were true and that the charges of involvement by members of the White House staff were false. The comments I made during this period, and the comments made by my Press Secretary on my behalf, were based on the information provided to us at the time we made those comments. However, new information then came to me which persuaded me that there was a real possibility that some of these charges were true, and suggesting further that there had been an effort to conceal the facts both from the public, from you, and from me.

As a result, on March 21, I personally assumed the responsibility for coordinating intensive new inquiries into the matter, and I personally ordered those conducting the investigations to get all the facts and to report them directly to me, right here in this office.

I again ordered that all persons in the Government or at the Reelection Committee should cooperate fully with the FBI, the prosecutors and the Grand Jury. I also ordered that anyone who refused to cooperate in telling the truth would be asked to resign from government service. And, with ground rules adopted that would preserve the basic constitutional separation of powers between the Congress and the Presidency, I directed that members of the White House staff should appear and testify voluntarily under oath before the Senate Committee investigating Watergate.

I was determined that we should get to the bottom of the matter, and that the truth should be fully brought out—no matter who was involved.

At the same time, I was determined not to take precipitate action, and to avoid, if at all possible, any action that would appear to reflect on innocent people. I wanted to be fair. But I knew that in the final analysis, the integrity of this office—public faith in the integrity of this office—would have to take priority over all personal considerations.

Today, in one of the most difficult decisions of my Presidency, I accepted the resignations of two of my closest associates in the White House—Bob Haldeman, John Ehrlichman—two of the finest public servants it has been my privilege to know.

I want to stress that in accepting these resignations, I mean to leave no implication whatever of personal wrongdoing on their part, and I leave no implication tonight of implication on the part of others who have been charged in this matter. But in matters as sensitive as guarding the integrity of our democratic process, it is essential not only that rigorous legal and ethical standards be observed, but also that the public, you, have total confidence that they are both being observed and enforced by those in authority and particularly by the President of the United States. They agreed with me that this move was necessary in order to restore that confidence.

Because Attorney General Kleindienst—though a distinguished public servant, my personal friend for twenty years, with no personal involvement whatever in this matter—has been a close personal and professional associate of some of those who are involved in this case, he and I both felt that it was also necessary to name a new Attorney General.

The Counsel to the President, John Dean, has also resigned.

As the new Attorney General, I have today named Elliot Richardson, a man of unimpeachable integrity and rigorously high principle. I have directed him to do everything necessary to ensure that the Department of Justice has the confidence and trust of every law-abiding person in this country.

I have given him absolute authority to make all decisions bearing upon the prosecution of the Watergate case and related matters. I have instructed him that if he should consider it appropriate, he has the authority to name a special supervising prosecutor for matters arising out of the case.

Whatever may appear to have been the case before—whatever improper activities may yet be discovered in connection with this whole sordid affair—I want the American people, I want you to know beyond the shadow of a doubt that during my terms as President, justice will be pursued fairly, fully and impartially, no matter who is involved. This office is a sacred trust and I am determined to be worthy of that trust.

Looking back at the history of this case, two questions arise:

How could it have happened?

Who is to blame?

Political commentators have correctly observed that during my twenty-seven years in politics I have always previously insisted on running my own campaigns for office.

But 1972 presented a very different situation. In both domestic and foreign policy, 1972 was a year of crucially important decisions, of intense negotiations, of vital new directions, particularly in working toward the goal which has been my overriding concern throughout my political career

—the goal of bringing peace to America and peace to the world.

That is why I decided, as the 1972 campaign approached, that the Presidency should come first and politics second. To the maximum extent possible, therefore, I sought to delegate campaign operations, and to remove the day-to-day campaign decisions from the President's office and from the White House. I also, as you recall, severely limited the number of my own campaign appearances.

Who, then, is to blame for what happened in this case?

For specific criminal actions by specific individuals, those who committed those actions, must, of course, bear the liability and pay the penalty.

For the fact that alleged improper actions took place within the White House or within my campaign organization, the easiest course would be for me to blame those to whom I delegated the responsibility to run the campaign. But that would be a cowardly thing to do.

I will not place the blame on subordinates—on people whose zeal exceeded their judgment, and who may have done wrong in a cause they deeply believed to be right.

In any organization, the man at the top must bear the responsibility. That responsibility, therefore, belongs here, in this office. I accept it. And I pledge to you tonight, from this office, that I will do everything in my power to ensure that the guilty are brought to justice, and that such abuses are purged from our political processes in the years to come, long after I have left this office.

Some people, quite properly appalled at the abuses that occurred, will say that Watergate demonstrates the bankruptcy of the American political system. I believe precisely the opposite is true. Watergate represented a series of illegal acts and bad judgments by a number of individuals. It was the system that has brought the facts to light and that will bring those guilty to justice—a system that in this case has included a determined Grand Jury, honest prosecutors, a courageous Judge, John Sirica, and a vigorous free press.

It is essential now that we place our faith in that system —and especially in the judicial system. It is essential that we let the judicial process go forward, respecting those safeguards that are established to protect the innocent as well as to convict the guilty. It is essential that in reacting to the excesses of others, we not fall into excesses ourselves.

It is also essential that we not be so distracted by events such as this that we neglect the vital work before us, before this Nation, before America, at a time of critical importance to America and the world.

Since March, when I first learned that the Watergate affair might in fact be far more serious than I had been led to believe, it has claimed far too much of my own time and attention.

Whatever may now transpire in the case—whatever the actions of the Grand Jury, whatever the outcome of any eventual trials—I must now turn my full attention once again to the larger duties of this office. I owe it to this great office that I hold, and I owe it to you—to our country.

I know that as Attorney General, Elliot Richardson will be both fair and fearless in pursuing this case wherever it leads. I am confident that with him in charge, justice will be done.

There is vital work to be done toward our goal of a lasting structure of peace in the world—work that cannot wait. Work that I must do.

Tomorrow, for example, Chancellor Brandt of West Germany will visit the White House for talks that are a vital element of "The Year of Europe" as 1973 has been called. We are already preparing for the next Soviet-American summit meeting, later this year.

This is also a year in which we are seeking to negotiate a mutual and balanced reduction of armed forces in Europe, which will reduce our defense budget and allow us to have funds for other purposes at home so desperately needed. It is the year when the United States and Soviet negotiators will seek to work out the second and even more important round of our talks on limiting nuclear arms, and of reducing the danger of a nuclear war that would destroy civilization as we know it. It is a year in which we confront the difficult tasks of maintaining peace in Southeast Asia, and in the potentially explosive Middle East.

There is also vital work to be done right here in America —to ensure prosperity, and that means a good job for everyone who wants to work, to control inflation, that I know worries every housewife, everyone who tries to balance a family budget in America, to set in motion new and better ways of ensuring progress toward a better life for all Americans.

When I think of this office—of what it means—I think of all the things that I want to accomplish for this nation—of all the things I want to accomplish for you.

On Christmas Eve, during my terrible personal ordeal of the renewed bombing of North Vietnam, which after twelve years of war, finally helped to bring America peace with honor, I sat down just before midnight. I wrote out some of my goals for my second term as President.

Let me read them to you.

"To make it possible for our children, and for our children's children, to live in a world of peace.

"To make this country be more than ever a land of opportunity—of equal opportunity, full opportunity for every American.

"To provide jobs for all who can work, and generous help for all who cannot.

"To establish a climate of decency, and civility, in which each person respects the feelings and the dignity and the God-given rights of his neighbor.

"To make this a land in which each person can dare to dream, can live his dreams—not in fear, but in hope—proud of his community, proud of his country, proud of what America has meant to himself and to the world."

These are great goals. I believe we can, we must work for them. We can achieve them. But we cannot achieve these goals unless we dedicate ourselves to another goal.

We must maintain the integrity of the White House, and that integrity must be real, not transparent. There can be no whitewash at the White House.

We must reform our political process—ridding it not only of the violations of the law, but also of the ugly mob violence, and other inexcusable campaign tactics that have been too often practiced and too readily accepted in the past—including those that may have been a response by one side to the excesses or expected excesses of the other side. Two wrongs do not make a right.

I have been in public life for more than a quarter of a century. Like any other calling, politics has good people, and bad people. And let me tell you, the great majority in politics, in the Congress, in the Federal Government, in the State Government, are good people. I know that it can be very easy, under the intensive pressures of a campaign, for even well-intentioned people to fall into shady tactics—to rationalize this on the grounds that what is at stake is of such importance to the Nation that the end justifies the means. And both of our great parties have been guilty of such tactics in the past.

In recent years, however, the campaign excesses that have occurred on all sides have provided a sobering demonstration of how far this false doctrine can take us. The lesson is clear: America, in its political campaigns, must not again fall into the trap of letting the end, however great that end is, justify the means.

I urge the leaders of both political parties, I urge citizens, all of you, everywhere, to join in working toward a new set of standards, new rules and procedures—to ensure that future elections will be as nearly free of such abuses as they possibly can be made. This is my goal. I ask you to join in making it America's goal.

When I was inaugurated for a second term this past January 20, I gave each member of my Cabinet and each member of my senior White House staff a special four-year calendar, with each day marked to show the number of days remaining to the Administration. In the inscription on each calendar, I wrote these words: "The Presidential term which begins today consists of 1,461 days—no more, no less. Each can be a day of strengthening and renewal for America; each can add depth and dimension to the American experience. If we strive together, if we make the most of the challenge and the opportunity that these days offer us, they can stand out as great days for America, and great moments in the history of the world."

I looked at my own calendar this morning up at Camp David as I was working on this speech. It showed exactly 1,361 days remaining in my term. I want these to be the best days in America's history, because I love America. I deeply believe that America is the hope of the world, and I know that in the quality and wisdom of the leadership America gives lies the only hope for millions of people all over the world, that they can live their lives in peace and freedom. We must be worthy of that hope, in every sense of the word. Tonight, I ask for your prayers to help me in everything that I do throughout the days of my Presidency to be worthy of their hopes and of yours.

God bless America and God bless each and every one of you.

TRUTH IN GOVERNMENT [5]

CHARLES McC. MATHIAS, JR. [6]

"The only way to restore confidence and trust throughout our society is for everyone who shares the privilege of leadership to obey the law and to meet the small questions and the great issues with equal courage," Charles McCurdy Mathias, Republican Senator from Maryland, told the Senate in a short speech April 17, 1973. The lawmaker delivered his pungent remarks extemporaneously, using only "long-hand notes." Like many other Senate presentations, this speech probably caused little stir on the floor of the Senate. But Senator Mathias did attract attention elsewhere. James Reston of the New York *Times* devoted an editorial to the speech and a long excerpt was published on the editorial page (May 4, 1973). The Senator received nearly two hundred letters expressing approval, from Maryland and from the entire country. His emphasis upon the simple virtue of honesty was refreshing and timely.

Mr. President, no danger that faces the United States today is more serious than the possibility that a significant number of our people are losing faith in the validity and purpose of our Government. The polls tell us of the growing distrust of the public in the honesty of public officials. That, in turn, leaches confidence in our institutions. I regard a temper of doubt or distrust as a great danger.

When a democratic government is imperilled by loss of confidence, it follows that the people must feel some lack of confidence in themselves. Corrosion attacks throughout the whole system. The challenge to leadership is then the restoration of trust in government and the renewal of faith in the Nation.

[5] Speech delivered in the United States Senate, April 17, 1973. Text in *Congressional Record,* April 17, 1973, p S6102-6103. Quoted by permission.

[6] For biographical note, see Appendix.

It is, therefore, useful to think a minute about the nature of loyalty and of simple patriotism. Each of us in Congress, and every other public official from the President to the most junior civil servant, has expressed his loyalty in its most elemental form when he took his oath to defend the Constitution. I believe that every one of us understood that the obligation of this oath was paramount to any other claim on us. No longer are we free to prefer the interest of a person or a party over the mandate of the Constitution. Loyalty in America is loyalty to the law of the land. The great inheritance from our Revolution is the freedom to choose this loyalty above all others.

Yet, it seems to me that at this moment the issue of conflicting loyalties is presented to us in three distinct cases that are pending in the Senate and demanding determination. The common question that must be answered in all three is whether the persons involved gave a greater loyalty to some lesser interest than to the Constitution. It is in this light that we have to make our separate judgment in the instances of the resurfacing of ITT as an influence on foreign policy, the nomination of L. Patrick Gray III to be Director of the Federal Bureau of Investigation, and in the investigation of Watergate election abuses.

The very fact that we are required to make judgments in these cases imposes upon us the identical choices that lay before the parties who are involved in each. We, ourselves, have to decide what is loyalty to the law, what is defense of the Constitution; and what is simply the strong pull of friendship, partisanship, or some veiled interest.

Such a choice seems simple when it is presented as an academic proposition; but each specific case bristles with practical problems and subordinate questions. Not the least of the cautions we must observe is the fact that loyalty to the law imposes adherence to the principle that every man is innocent until he is proven otherwise. Unjust accusations can no more be tolerated in the Senate than unjust actions can be condoned.

Our responsibilities are great, our difficulties are great, but whether our work will be great depends on whether we, ourselves, are inspired by the impartial spirit of the Constitution and whether we can accurately communicate it to our fellow countrymen.

In this task our only tool is truth. And it is truth that usually suffers first when loyalties are divided. No person who is involved or engaged in the life of his generation can avoid the competing demands of his family, his friends, his business or his State. If he gives equal priority to each, or revolving priority to the most pressing, his life will undoubtedly be chaotic. But if he, in his personal life, as we in our national life, establishes some order, he can expect to live in peace and security. It is when we are tempted to ignore the priorities of our obligations that we get into trouble. We trifle with the truth.

Some years ago, the official spokesman for the Department of Defense, Assistant Secretary Arthur Sylvester, attempted to legitimize the practice, in which the Department had presumably been engaged, of lying to the people of the United States in the name of their Government. The result was as disastrous as it was predictable. Popular understanding and support for the war in Vietnam was not increased; on the contrary, it was seriously undermined. Even after several changes in administration in the Pentagon, its credibility has not been fully restored.

Consider, on the other hand, the example of Winston Churchill in the Battle of Britain. As Walter Lippmann has pointed out, Churchill demonstrated his faith in democracy by sharing the truth with his people.

No matter how bad the news, no matter how serious the situation, no matter how desperate the danger, Churchill not only faced the truth but he told it. The result was not despair in Britain but rather renewed confidence in the Prime Minister, in his government, and in the ultimate values of the British Constitution, which made winning worthwhile.

And so I say again that the pursuit of truth is the only direction in which we can go in search of the way to preserve our loyalty to the Constitution and the laws. A visible, unshakeable demonstration of that loyalty is the only way I know to restore the confidence, hope, and aspiration that many of us find missing in our national life today.

We are more likely to reach this goal if we candidly admit the obstacles in our way. It is very human to want to do a favor for a friend or an errand for an organization, or perhaps to keep our powder dry for another occasion which may or may not happen. But these are temptations that we share with all humanity and so we need not be ashamed of being tempted, but only of succumbing and betraying our prime loyalty.

It will be asked, I am sure, why I have taken the time to philosophize in this way without adding any new or dramatic element to the continuing debate. I did so because I think the pervasive problem of confusion of loyalties has poisoned public ethical behavior and hit at the heart of scepticism about Government and politics. I am tired of hearing about how "they all do it in Washington" and I want to hear more of "it may have been that way once, but it is not that way anymore."

The only way to restore confidence and trust throughout our society is for everyone who shares the privilege of leadership to obey the law, and to meet the small questions and the great issues with equal courage.

We shall need the encouragement of concerned citizens. We shall need the cooperation and the candor of those who share power with us at every level of government. We shall need to discipline ourselves to a kind of objectivity that rejects partisanship whether we are cast in the role of prosecutor or defender in any given case. We shall need to reaffirm the strength of our own moral fiber and the influence of conscience on the course of our lives.

But I have faith in the healing strength of truth. I have confidence that we can prove again that for men and women everywhere America is still the last best hope on Earth.

WOMEN IN POLITICS

MEET THE PRESS [1]

GLORIA STEINEM AND JILL RUCKELSHAUS [2]

"This is the year of the woman. In the political past, tokenism has been their fate. But this year there are rumblings of change in the parties," said Katie Louchheim of *The Christian Science Monitor* (Des Moines *Register,* May 28, 1972). This prediction was borne out at the two political conventions in Miami. Thirty-eight percent of the delegates to the Democratic convention were women, many of whom were having their "first go" at politics and attending a national convention. Furthermore, Jean Westwood became national chairwoman of the Democratic party. Likewise there was increased female representation and participation, working to involve women in the Republican convention. The National Women's Political Caucus exerted pressure on both parties to send women delegates to the meetings.

Following the two conventions, NBC's "Meet the Press: America's Press Conference of the Air," turned its attention to women in politics on its program of September 10, 1972. Lawrence E. Spivak, producer of the program for many years, served as moderator. The women interviewed were two members of the Policy Council of the National Women's Political Caucus: Gloria Steinem, writer and editor of *Ms.* magazine, representing the Democrats, and Jill Ruckelshaus, wife of the former administrator of the Environmental Protection Agency, representing the Republicans. The two women were questioned by Carl T. Rowan of the Chicago *Daily News,* Shana Alexander of *Newsweek,* James J. Kilpatrick of the Washington *Star* Syndicate, and Catherine Mackin of NBC News.

The ensuing discussion revealed the concerns of the two women about female participation in the policy making and the future goals of the advocates of women's rights. By their answers, the two interviewees suggested that they were intent upon presenting a united front and upon pushing their mutual concerns. Nevertheless, their divergent views were also quite evident. Mrs.

[1] Interviews presented over NBC Network, Sunday, September 10, 1972. Quoted by permission.

[2] For biographical notes, see Appendix.

Ruckelshaus had a more difficult position to maintain because she had to defend what the Republicans had done during the first Nixon term and she had less concrete evidence of active involvement of women at the Republican convention.

The two women were well chosen. Ms. Steinem has spoken and written much on women's rights and in fact made a forceful speech during the Democratic convention.

Mrs. Ruckelshaus, the wife of a prominent moderate Republican, was much in evidence at the Republican convention and was interviewed several times during the Republican proceedings. Later President Nixon appointed her Assistant to the Counsel for Women's Programs. Both women are effective speakers, direct and poised.

MR. SPIVAK: Our guests today are two members of the Policy Council of the National Women's Political Caucus: Gloria Steinem, who was the Caucus Spokeswoman to the Democratic Convention, and Jill Ruckelshaus, who was the Spokeswoman to the Republican Convention.

The Caucus was founded in 1971 to win greater participation for women in national affairs and to elect more women to public office.

Ms. Steinem is a writer and the editor of the feminist magazine, *Ms.*

Mrs. Ruckelshaus, a former teacher, is the mother of five children. Her husband is Administrator of the Environmental Protection Agency.

MR. ROWAN: Ms. Steinem, back during the primaries you referred to Senator George McGovern as "the best of the white male candidates." Are you satisfied with the stand he took at the convention and since with regard to women's rights?

MS. STEINEM: No, I am not completely satisfied with them, but I still consider them the most hopeful. Obviously, from the convention it is clear that the women there, the majority of the women there, were displeased with the fact that a minority plank on reproductive freedom was not included. We considered it unwise politically since the majority of Americans and the majority of Catholic Americans as well are in favor of that, but that was the only major request that was made by the National Women's Political Caucus for inclusion in the platform that was not met.

MR. ROWAN: At one time you said that "revolution, not reform," is what is needed. On the basis of what you saw at the Democratic Convention do you now think women can win rights by working through the political system?

MS. STEINEM: I think we have to use a variety of methods. It was clear to me that our gains in 1972 had a great deal to do with the implicit threat of another 1968, so we can't neglect the ways in which demonstrations and other kinds of techniques influence the changes that are made. In other words, we need a multiplicity of tactics in order to get changes within the system.

MR. ROWAN: Mrs. Ruckelshaus, you were at the Republican Convention. Are you convinced that the Republican party has now made a firm commitment to women's equality?

MRS. RUCKELSHAUS: Yes, I am convinced of that. I think that there were some confusion, some failure to fully understand the commitment of the women in the party to recognition of the right of women to participate as full partners in society. We went a long way in August in Miami Beach in convincing the leadership, both men and women, in the party, that the women throughout the country who are Republicans and who are Independents and who are Democrats are committed to winning these rights for themselves, that they will choose the party which offers them the greatest opportunity. I think our party woke up to that fact, and I think their commitment now is quite firm.

MR. ROWAN: One of your colleagues, Betty Friedan, said that the GOP was trying to rip off the Women's Political Caucus, that they were using you and the Political Caucus. Was this an unfair charge?

MRS. RUCKELSHAUS: I don't think that was quite accurate. She was quibbling over a choice of words. The Republican National Committee had a seminar on women's issues, which they called the Republican Women's Political Caucus. As a matter of fact, I think I might have been responsible for choosing those words. There was no attempt to usurp the function of the National Women's Political Caucus.

Ms. STEINEM: I would like to say in solidarity here that there is a Democratic Women's Political Caucus too, so there is clearly no partisan attempt to use those words unfairly.

MR. ROWAN: Mrs. Ruckelshaus, Senator McGovern charges that President Nixon has treated the women's movement as a joke. What is your response to that charge?

MRS. RUCKELSHAUS: I think we will be hearing a lot of charges and countercharges in that vein. I think that is not true. The Republican party has established a good record on women's opportunities, women's rights and responsibilities during the last four years. Surely it is a step forward from anything that preceded it. It is not enough. There will be more. The party is committed in a very strong women's plank in this convention platform to being sure that women are included, that women are given positions of leadership.

I don't think that is a fair charge, but I am sure we will hear others like it during the campaign, and it will be up to women to be alert as to what the facts are as opposed to what the rhetoric is.

Ms. ALEXANDER: Ms. Steinem, I think we would all agree with you that the women's movement has made greater progress in the last year or two than in the fifty years since women got the vote, but since it is a militant movement, I would like to ask you, as you see it, who is the enemy now?

Ms. STEINEM: I wouldn't call it a militant movement, because "militant" connotes violence, and to me, I would more likely call the Pentagon a militant movement. It is part of feminist philosophy, as you know, to be—in fact women's culture is much less violent per se than the men's culture per se, but the adversary, which is the word that I prefer to enemy, are those individuals who have usurped control of our lives, and who in general turn out to be that

3 percent of the population which is white, male, over thirty and college educated. That is the pool from which we have taken our leadership in fact, which I think goes a long way to explaining the poverty of the leadership.

Ms. Alexander: Are you saying that the white, male, educated person is the enemy of the women's movement, or the adversary, I beg your pardon?

Ms. Steinem: From a statistical point of view that is accurate. I mean the surveys that have been done of reaction to the women's movement show that that group of people socially upward, mobile, and so on, shows the most resistance to the movement because they have the most privilege to lose. However, the overall point is that this is a humanist movement, and that, of course, those individuals, even that 3 percent, have a great deal to gain. I hope that soon they will realize—I think some individuals have realized it—that the male role is also very restrictive and dehumanizing and that they themselves have a great deal to gain by this social revolution.

Mr. Kilpatrick: Mrs. Ruckelshaus, Senator McGovern many times has promised that if elected he would appoint or nominate to the United States Supreme Court a woman. Mr. Nixon has made no such promise from his side. What is your impression of Senator McGovern's promise? Will that win votes for the Democratic nominee?

Mrs. Ruckelshaus: I am sure that he is sincere in that statement. I don't question that at all. I am not certain that that will end up winning votes for him. There is a statement in the women's plank in the Republican National Party Platform which urges the party to appoint women to policy-making positions in the government, including the Supreme Court and the Cabinet. I feel very confident that if the President is reelected we will have women in the Cabinet and on the Supreme Court during his second four-year term. I am not sure that either candidate will be able to capture the women's vote on the basis of promises.

MR. KILPATRICK: I had understood you to say a moment ago that you felt the women would go with the candidate who made the greatest appeal to them along these lines.

MRS. RUCKELSHAUS: Yes, but appeal is not based on promise. I am a Republican, and I will support the President on the basis of his performance, and during the past four years he has moved women forward through legal directives to his agencies and departments that they have action plans for hiring and promoting women, through his insistence that outside organizations that make contracts with the federal government submit action plans, through his appointment of women to policy-making jobs treble the ratio of any previous administration. This is positive performance, this is not promise.

MR. KILPATRICK: Mrs. Ruckelshaus, I have heard it said those figures are a little bit phony, that they have to do with grade levels under civil service, and by comparing it in this administration against that on a different basis, it makes the Nixon administration look good. What is your response to that?

MRS. RUCKELSHAUS: My response is that I am really not interested in the percentages. I think that that argument can be made, perhaps even substantiated. It is clear that more has happened for women to enable women to achieve their full responsibilities and rights under this administration than the previous one. No administration can step back from that. This administration, if it continues four years, will go forward. The administration is not the only one which might have done it in this four-year period, but that is a record of performance upon which the Republican party can proudly stand.

MR. SPIVAK: Ms. Steinem, do you feel you have something to say?

MS. STEINEM: The point of the Caucus is to put forth women's issues and women's concerns, and it is a multi-partisan organization. We are especially grateful, I am personally grateful, to the women in the Republican party who are there struggling, and the majority of the women in the Caucus in fact are neither Republicans nor Democrats, but are Independents.

We have to admit though that the record of this administration is not so much a tribute to this administration as a testimony to the poverty that has gone before, because those 118 women, as you say, have been pointed out by the federally employed women here as a very dubious statistic, as they include President Nixon's personal secretary, women in the military who got, you know, fairly routine promotions, and the like. So we really have to look at that very, very carefully and understand that in the government as elsewhere the women are still the first to be fired and the last to be hired, and they still constitute a very, very small minority of people there at all, and the vast majority, 75 percent, are in grades one to six which, of course, are clerical roles.

Miss Mackin: Ms. Steinem, if we could just go back and relive the Democratic Convention for a minute here. The women were outmaneuvered twice by the McGovern people: once on the South Carolina vote and once on the abortion issue. In retrospect, do you think there is anything at all you and the National Women's Political Caucus could have done about that?

Ms. Steinem: I don't know really. I think there was a nervousness about the numerical problem, which was so complex because it so directly affected the California challenge. I am not sure we could have done anything to calm that nervousness. It is clear it would have been technically possible to support the women's challenge in that case. As for reproductive freedom, I repeat, I think that is a poor political judgment, because it simply doesn't reflect the way the majority of Americans feel, and it was showing a sensitivity to a small and very vocal pressure group that McGovern would clearly not allow to happen when it comes to the war, for instance. But it was an enormous victory, I think, for the women in both parties, that these issues were raised, that women's issues were probably the most exciting and the most—showed the most forward thrust of any issues at either convention.

MISS MACKIN: Would you go along with those people who said it was more important to nominate McGovern than it was for women to face down these issues, for instance, on South Carolina, and on abortion?

MS. STEINEM: No, I think the issues are more important than any candidate.

MR. SPIVAK: Ms. Steinem, may I ask you a question? You made a speech before the National Press Club this year, and you said: "Women are not taken seriously. We are undervalued, ridiculed or ignored by society, which consciously and unconsciously assumes that the white male is the standard and the norm."

What is your explanation for this serious state of affairs, in view of the fact that men—males—are at least virtually controlled and dominated by women from birth to puberty and often beyond that? Why haven't you done a better job, if you are as smart as you say you are?

MS. STEINEM: That is your statement, not mine, that men are virtually controlled by women from birth onward. I mean, if you take a very intelligent person with the normal hopes and ambitions and confine her to the home, she becomes sometimes over-dominating within those four walls, as a man would be as well. But the truth of her situation is that she has no real power over her life outside the home, nor does she have power over the economics, over the politics of her life. So, you know, I wouldn't accept the premise of that statement.

MR. SPIVAK: Hasn't she an opportunity to brainwash the male during those early formative years? Why doesn't she do it?

MS. STEINEM: I think it is beginning to change, not to brainwash, but to be objective for a change and to eliminate the sex and the race stereotypes, but women have been encouraged to invest their hopes and their dreams in their male children and convinced that their female children could not meet those expectations, to depend on their male children in their old age and so on, and have been made to realize the rather severe danger and risk in not perpetuating the small amount of well-being that they have in the system as it is. What kind of choice is it, after all, to be able to go out and earn half as much as a man for doing exactly the same work? Could she support her family? Could she support her children? Should she tell her daughter that she could? I think not.

Ms. Alexander: Mrs. Ruckelshaus, the latest Gallup poll indicated that two out of three Americans believe that abortion is a matter to be decided between a woman and her physician, and yet both political candidates seem to be ducking that issue completely. Would that lead you to conclude that the people are more for abortion than the practical politician?

Mrs. Ruckelshaus: That is the conclusion I would reach, yes. I think the public is way out in front of the politicians on this issue. The politicians have listened, I think, probably to the intensity of the argument rather than to the diversity of the argument, the widespread support of freedom of the woman to make that decision, that very personal decision in consultation with her own conscience and her physician rather than being restricted by a state law.

Mr. Rowan: Ms. Steinem, this issue of abortion, or reproductive freedom, seems to be one of the burning issues among women in your group. What, specifically, is it you want? Do you want to wipe out all the bans and state-imposed prohibitions on abortion?

Ms. Steinem: Yes. The position of the Caucus is one against government intervention in the reproductive freedom of the individual citizen. That affects men as well as women. It means birth control as well as abortion. It also means the enforced sterilization laws which exist in many states in this country and which affect criminals and any individuals considered socially undesirable. It very often affects poor and minority people, welfare clients and the like. It is clear from the opinions in other industrialized countries, and also from the opinions here, that that is not—the wish of the average citizen, male and female, is not to have government intervention in that most private area of personal freedom.

MISS MACKIN: Mrs. Ruckelshaus, recently President Nixon has taken strong positions against quotas, and it would seem to me the way I interpret it, anything that can be construed as something that approaches a quota, which might also include "positive action," a thing that has been used to end discrimination. Do you think the President's position on this will adversely affect women's advancement in the society?

MRS. RUCKELSHAUS: No, I don't think so. As a woman who has perfect confidence in women to achieve their representation based on their quality as well as their quantity, which happens to be over 50 percent of the population, I am not concerned that, if given an equal start, we won't eventually find ourselves well represented at the finish line. I don't think the President has said that there shouldn't be equal representation according to ability.

MISS MACKIN: But the positive action is something that has been used throughout the sixties to get black people into the system and to a more limited extent to get women into the system, so if that is removed, what are we left with?

MRS. RUCKELSHAUS: That wasn't removed. That was the basis for which a lot of juggling at the Republican Convention, and in a certain rule, which asked that succeeding conventions would endeavor to have equal representation of women, the term "positive action" was left in to say that the party must go out and include minorities, old people, young people and women.

Miss Mackin: That has to do with the Republican party. What I am talking about is the society at large. The Philadelphia Plan, which the President has taken a very strong position on, vis-à-vis, black people, but also if you carry that over to women, that is what I am asking you, whether or not you think this will keep women from advancing?

Mrs. Ruckelshaus: No. I don't see that—you know I am not clear on where you think the term "positive action" has been used to keep women from achieving their equal representation.

Miss Mackin: Positive action has been used as the legal means to involve people who are discriminated against.

Mrs. Ruckelshaus: Where has that been removed? Where has the President—

Miss Mackin: It has been used in industry. Mostly in industry, especially for black people and to a more limited extent for women.

Mr. Spivak: Mrs. Ruckelshaus, will you answer that question first, or that statement?

Mrs. Ruckelshaus: I would like to say with the eventual ratification of the ERA [Equal Rights Amendment] that many of those problems and those worries will be legitimately taken care of through the Constitutional Amendment.

Mr. Spivak: Mrs. Ruckelshaus, a New York *Post* article quoted you as saying "Republican women are different; they are not as vocal or as emotional as the Democrats." If you were accurately quoted, what is your explanation for the difference between women Democrats and women Republicans?

Mrs. Ruckelshaus: I am not sure I can really explain that. I think I was accurately quoted, and I think I do believe that. I am not sure I can explain it. Maybe it is what leads them into either party in the first place.

I do know that our approach at the Republican Convention was quite different than the approach the Caucus women made at the Democratic Convention. Yet we both achieved, I think, a very high level of success with our independent approaches as women, and both parties were responsive to the separate approaches that were used.

MR. SPIVAK: We have less than four minutes now.

MR. KILPATRICK: Following up on Mr. Rowan's question of a moment ago, does the Caucus also want to see all the laws against prostitution abolished?

MS. STEINEM: There is no position on prostitution per se, but when we talk about equalizing the laws, obviously that would have that effect, but I think we do have to say relative to the questions that we were just answering, the point is that the Republican women, for instance, in the area of child care, had to deal with an administration which had just vetoed a child development bill. The Democratic women had to deal with a group already wedded to the idea of child care in general, so I think we are talking about relativity of the struggle, and that is why we are a part of one organization supporting each other and so on, but it would be unfair to leave the viewer with the impression that the women's plank in the area of child care and other areas were the same. They are not the same.

MR. KILPATRICK: On the matter of the Equal Rights Amendment, the criticism is made that that is wonderful for you as a professional woman, but it doesn't do a thing on earth for the woman who works in a factory or in a home. How do you respond to that?

MS. STEINEM: That is wildly inaccurate, and I am afraid that is a case of the unions using, in the name of poor women, speaking against an Equal Rights Amendment, which will in fact help poor women very, very much. They have often wanted to maintain their so-called protective labor legislation in order to keep jobs within the union as a male province. In fact, they are being knocked down state by state under the Fourteenth Amendment anyway, so the truth of that point of view would leave women without the protective legislation and without the Equal Rights Amendment.

It is clear it is in the interests of the poor women, and the women of UAW and other unions agree, to pass the Equal Rights Amendment with all speed.

MR. ROWAN: Mrs. Ruckelshaus, some feminists say that it is the very institution of marriage itself that enslaves women and that there won't be any real freedom for women until that is wiped out. Is that an argument that you accept?

MRS. RUCKELSHAUS: No, it isn't. I think what this movement is about is the full expression of a woman's potential, and that includes for many women a husband and a family. But that is not the full expression. The husband and family cannot be the full expression. I think many women stop short of their own evolution when they think they have reached their capacity, when they are married and are raising a family.

MR. ROWAN: There are some other people who say even talking about this gives the women's rights movement a bad name. Do you think it is bad for them to talk about wiping out the institution of marriage?

MRS. RUCKELSHAUS: Oh, I don't think so. I think there are many people who are responsive to that argument. To another large segment of the woman population, of which I am a member, the institution of marriage is a very important part of my life, but it is not the entire reason for my being, Mr. Rowan.

MR. SPIVAK: We have less than a minute.

MS. ALEXANDER: Ms. Steinem, there has been a lot of talk about you, yourself, going actively into politics. Do you have some plans?

MS. STEINEM: No, I have no such plans, but I look forward to working for women who are strong on women's issues and the issues of all powerless groups. I enjoy working at that, but I am much more comfortable with the typewriter than here in public.

MS. ALEXANDER: You have no plans of running for elective office?

Ms. Steinem: No.

Mr. Spivak: I am sorry to interrupt, but our time is almost up, and we won't be able to get in another question or an answer.

Thank you, Ms. Steinem, and Mrs. Ruckelshaus, for being with us today on "Meet The Press."

WOMEN IN POLITICS[3]

SHIRLEY CHISHOLM[4]

On February 9, 1973, Representative Shirley Chisholm, Democrat of New York, addressed the eight hundred delegates who attended the National Women's Political Caucus meeting in the Grand Ballroom of the Rice Hotel in Houston. Ranging in age from seventeen to seventy-three, the listeners came from all parts of the nation and represented all political complexions, from radical feminists to middle-class members of the League of Women Voters. Among Mrs. Chisholm's listeners were some of the most prominent women leaders in the country, including Liz Carpenter, Gloria Steinem, Pat Schroeder, Bella Abzug, Mary Coleman, and Frances T. Farenthold.

Shirley Chisholm came with excellent credentials. She had made a much admired bid for the Democratic presidential nomination. Although she was never regarded as a serious threat to the front-runners, she gained much favorable national exposure and won millions of admirers for her directness, dignity, and good sense. Furthermore, in the election she won reelection to the House in her New York district, garnering 87.6 percent of the vote, against three opponents.

Shirley Chisholm is a most effective speaker. She stands erect, uses excellent language, and is direct and persuasive. Schooled in rugged political speaking in New York City, she is able to build rapport and to meet an audience on its own ground. She is equally effective before women's groups, black groups, street rallies, college assemblies, the National Democratic Convention, or the House of Representatives. She is adept in extemporaneous and impromptu situations and knows how to cope with the questions of reporters. She is among the best women speakers on the American scene today. (See her speech "Economic Injustice in America Today" in REPRESENTATIVE AMERICAN SPEECHES: 1971-1972, pages 27-36).

Well aware of the differences of opinion and goals among the delegates and of the frustration among the leaders, Representative Chisholm gave a straightforward keynote address which recommended unity and careful goal setting.

[3] Address delivered before the National Women's Political Caucus Convention, Houston, February 9, 1973. Quoted by permission.

[4] For biographical note, see Appendix.

When it was arranged that I should speak to you today, Liz Carpenter wrote me a note and suggested my speech should be, "Can a Woman Become President?" Knowing Liz, she probably thought this would be a wonderful occasion for me to exhort an audience of potential candidates to plan their own onslaughts on the pinnacle of elective office.

As I look back on the past year and a half, I think my campaign did help to break the barrier against women seeking the presidency and other elective offices but, my experiences also made me acutely aware of some of the problems women candidates face as well as particular problems which the women's movement, and especially the National Women's Political Caucus, must face up to.

One of my biggest problems was that my campaign was viewed as a symbolic gesture. While I realized that my campaign was an important rallying symbol for women and that my presence in the race forced the other candidates to deal with issues relating to women, my primary objective was to force people to accept me as a real viable candidate.

Although many have compared my race to that of Victoria Woodhull, I specifically rejected that comparison. Mrs. Woodhull was a feminist candidate running on a feminist party platform. I specifically rejected this feminist candidacy as I did the projection of myself into a black candidacy or an antiwar candidacy. I chose to run for the nomination of one of the major national parties.

I did this because I feel that the time for tokenism and symbolic gestures is past. Women need to plunge into the world of politics and battle it out toe to toe on the same ground as their male counterparts. If they do not do this, they will not succeed as a presidential candidate or in any other campaign for political office.

First and foremost, it is essential that you believe in yourself and your ability to handle the job you are seeking. If you don't, it is difficult to persuade others to support you. While pretty obvious to anyone who has run for office, I found that the press, the public, and even those in the women's movement found it difficult to understand this key point. Over and over in the campaign, I was asked, "But why are you running, Mrs. Chisholm?" Over and over I would reply, "Because I think I can do the job," "Because I think I am better than the rest of the candidates in the field."

One of the stumbling blocks I encountered was the fact that many people, including feminists, thought that since I "didn't have a chance" it was foolish to work for me.

For those who genuinely preferred another candidate, one can have no quarrel. But for those who thought I was the best candidate but chose to work for someone else because they viewed my campaign as hopeless, they will need to reexamine their thinking for truly, no woman will ever achieve the presidency as long as their potential supporters hold this view.

As the effect of the Wallace phenomenon in this last election points out, a campaign becomes truly effective when those who believe in their candidate pull out all the stops.

One of the other most difficult problems I faced was that many of my wonderful women's movement supporters did not understand that I both wanted and needed to talk about issues other than equal rights, abortion and child care. As you know, I am a strong supporter of all of these issues but in a campaign, there is a great deal of other ground to cover. Senior citizens don't really give a hang about abortion and homosexuals are more concerned with their own situation than the status of the Equal Rights Amendment.

Further, and this is critical to the discussion we will enter into at this convention, different women view different segments of the women's movement agenda as priority items.

The movement has, for the most part, been led by educated white middle-class women. There is nothing unusual about this. Reform as movements are usually led by the better educated and better off. But, if the women's movement is to be successful you must recognize the broad variety of women there are and the depth and range of their interests and concerns. To black and Chicano women, picketing a restricted club or insisting on the title Ms. are not burning issues. They are more concerned about bread-and-butter items such as the extension of minimum wage, welfare reform and day care.

Further, they are not only women but women of color and thus are subject to additional and sometimes different pressures.

For example, the black experience in America has not been one of unbridled success for black men. Indeed, there have been times when discrimination and the economic situation were such that it was easier for a black woman to get a job than her husband. Because of this, anything that might be construed as anti-male will be viewed skeptically by a black woman.

Indeed this is a problem not only for black women but most women.

If this caucus is to have a real impact, we must have a broad base and appeal to the average woman.

Unfortunately, the movement is currently perceived as anti-male, anti-child, and anti-family.

Part of this is bad press. The media does not concentrate on the blue-haired lady in pearls testifying on behalf of the equal employment opportunities bill. It trains its eyes on the young girl shaking her fist and screaming obscenities at an abortion rally.

Part of it is that many of the leaders of the movement have down-graded traditional roles in their attempts to show abuses and to affirm the right of a woman to have a choice of roles to play.

Finally, there have been excesses. Not all sexual advances are sexist. Children are more than a pile of dirty diapers, and families while they have often restricted women, have also provided warmth, security, and love.

If we are to succeed in uniting ourselves and in attracting the typical woman who is likely to be a housewife and mother who likes living in suburbia, we are going to have to make a concerted effort to articulate issues so that everyone will want to be identified with and active in the movement.

With this in mind, the function of the National Women's Political Caucus is not to be the cutting edge of the women's liberation movement but the big umbrella organization which provides the weight and muscle for those issues which the majority of women see as concerns.

One of the critical items on the convention agenda is to put the National Women's Political Caucus on a sound financial basis. I don't know if you realize it or not but most of the time the women in our national office have to pay for the privilege of being screamed at, accused of doing things without authorization, or not doing enough. Yet, in a real sense these gals are the Caucus. They get the mailings out, they do the nitty grittying of organizing meetings and conventions. Most of the time they work long hours and are lucky to get reimbursed for carfare. If we accuse others of ripping off and abusing women, we should begin by rectifying our own house.

It is time we rose above the cake sale mentality of financing. In this country we spend $6.4 billion on cosmetics. If we can spend that much on our faces, we can spend ten dollars a year for a membership fee—that is less than one dollar a month. Newsletters are also an enormous expense and should be put on some kind of paying basis.

Finally, we should set aside money to hire one full-time paid legislative lobbyist for the Caucus, and set up legislative lobbying leaders in every state and major subdivision. What is the point of having a National Women's Political Caucus and working at electing women to office if we ignore the simplest and most obvious methods of effecting this political process—that of lobbying? Without this we will lose everything we have gained. Right now the Equal Rights Amendment is stalled in the ratification process. Without effective lobbying, it will die after over a half a century of effort. The minimum wage bill, which affects a vast number of women was killed last year for a want of five votes to send it to conference committee. The National Women's Political Caucus could provide the margin of votes necessary for passage. After we passed a child care bill, the President vetoed it saying that day-care center were destructive to families. The White House needs to know this is a vital issue for women all over America and that we disagree.

Another issue this convention must grapple with is the form and format of this organization and the composition of the new policy council. I, for one, believe that the Caucus will never be completely effective unless we develop a strong grass roots organization.

As I traveled around the country, I met hundreds of bright, capable, articulate women. These are the people who ought to be projected into the positions of authority and leadership.

We don't need any more of the "superstar" syndrome. Indeed, I am sure that Betty, Gloria, and Bella are as sick of seeing their faces as I am of seeing mine. What we need is to thrust new people into the limelight and to show the range and breadth of talent among women all over the nation.

I, therefore, propose that you do not place my name in nomination for the policy council and I hope that the others in the policy council, who are in the same position, will do likewise. This does not mean breaking our association with the Caucus. You can establish some sort of honorary advisory council or hall of fame or something and we can remain "on call" when we are needed but, what is necessary now are new faces.

In closing, I would like to make one observation: normally our meetings go on endlessly with much shouting, haranguing, grandstanding, and discussion of extraneous issues. Could we all try to be respectful and understanding of each other's views, concise, to the point, and mindful of the clock.

YOU CAN DO IT [5]

Patricia Schroeder [6]

One of the six female newcomers to the United States House of Representatives is Patricia Schroeder, Democrat of Colorado. This young lawyer from Denver is the first woman to be sent to Congress from her state. In speaking of her victory—surprising even to herself—she recalls, "I never thought I would get out of the primary. Actually I never thought I would run for anything."

The Colorado congresswoman is active in the causes of women and is a member of NOW and the League of Women Voters. "Of course I'm for women's rights." She explains, "The only way we will get a higher equality of life is if everyone participates."

"Women have been told so often they can spectate and not participate," she feels, "that they have thought they are not capable of participating. But yes, we are." (*The Christian Science Monitor,* April 3, 1973) On February 25, 1973, she appeared on ABC's "Issues and Answers," as a "leading proponent" of the Equal Rights Amendment and opposite Mrs. Phyllis Schlafly, national chairman of Stop ERA, outspoken opponent of the amendment.

On February 9, 1973, Representative Schroeder spoke to the National Women's Political Caucus, at its meeting at the Rice Hotel in Houston. She gave a short speech in which she offered "a few suggestions from my own experience" on how to run successfully for office. In the talk, informative in tone, Mrs. Schroeder is most specific in her recommendations. She inserts into her development phrases that let the listener know that she is speaking from direct experience: "in my own case . . . ," "in our county nominating convention . . . ," "my husband often said . . . ," and "I was the only major candidate running." By such phrases, she establishes what is generally referred to as ethos, or credibility.

Senator Robert Kennedy once said of his brother, John, after the President's assassination, "If there is a lesson from his life and death, it is that in this world of ours, we can no

[5] Speech delivered at the National Women's Political Caucus, Houston, February 9, 1973. Quoted by permission.

[6] For biographical note, see Appendix.

longer be satisfied with being mere spectators, critics on the sidelines."

And surely that must be the continuing message for all of us here today. Women especially can no longer be mere spectators of the political process, critics on the sidelines; but active participants, playing an important and vital role out on the field.

By your presence here today, each of you is demonstrating her interest in the political process. Many of you have no doubt taken active roles in community and civic organizations, political activities and campaigns, or business and professional activities. You can *do* the job—but first, you have to *get* the job. For those of you, and I hope there are many, who may be contemplating a run for office—whether it be party, city, state, judicial, or federal—let me offer a few suggestions from my own experience.

First: Assess critically your own qualifications. It is probably fair to say—although certainly unfair in practice—that a woman running for public office should be "overqualified." Having been chairman of your church's women's club may not carry the same clout as being program chairman of the local Rotary Club.

It is interesting to note that all five of this years' new congresswomen are lawyers. Perhaps this is because, as lawyers, we have necessarily been thrust into an adverse, and often competitive, role with members of the male establishment. Furthermore, we have come into constant contact with many of the problems that face our communities, and worked on possible legislative solutions.

Second: Examine carefully the real base of your support. The support of one's family, close friends, and associates is indispensable. But what contacts, or qualifications do you have that will enable you to gain the confidence and backing of other groups and allies? In my own case, an extensive labor law background was valuable in helping eventually obtain both organizational and financial support from many labor unions. Teaching contacts with three major colleges in Denver were also important. Finally, it is essential to take the pulse, and constantly stroke the brows of many of the key party leaders and workers in your area. Many of these veterans of the political wars often will make astute judgements about prospective candidates. Every candidate honestly believes he or she is in fact *the* best candidate. If none of the pros agree, best reexamine your position.

Third: Build credibility. Because you are a woman, you will constantly confront the attitude that you are not "a serious candidate." At our County nominating convention it is customary for candidates to have booths, give away courtesy coffee, distribute literature, placard the walls with posters, etc. I had a basic feeling of aversion to that sort of thing; but we decided it was probably more important that I do some of the traditional things, simply because I was the untraditional candidate.

Because you are a woman you may have the ability to gain more than your fair share of press and media coverage, because you are the different candidate. But the other side of the coin is that you will often be more severely cross-examined on your views and statements by newspeople than is the average male candidate.

Fourth: Develop a strong "grassroots" organization. You will find that there are great reservoirs of dedicated, talented women who will really work for another woman. This is especially true of many older, retired women; and many younger gals, such as students and working girls.

You will probably have a very hard time raising money. My husband often said that the money "is controlled by male chauvinist pigs." Organization and union money is controlled by men, and they will usually have little confidence in the chances of a woman candidate. Hence, the bigger and better volunteer group you can muster, the better chance you will have of putting your scarce dollars into essential items like printed materials and media time.

Fifth: Use innovative and hard-hitting media. Because a woman candidate is "different," don't be afraid to run a different kind of campaign, utilizing original and different media techniques and content. Let me give you one example: the standard political brochure. You know what I am talking about—the picture of the candidate with family, with coat over the shoulder, in front of the Capitol, etc. with the standard one-liners: "X is honest; X is against pollution; X is for fiscal responsibility." We were able to achieve real impact—and also ruffle some feathers—with colorful mini-posters.

And finally, Sixth: Be issue-oriented. Running for public office is too time-consuming and too expensive to embark on such a venture merely for the experience, or for the ego satisfaction. If you run, take a stand. Get out front on the issues that concern you, your family, your community, and the nation. The risk, of course, is great; but so are the rewards.

And again, being a woman has both its advantages and disadvantages. I think a woman can more easily take a strong position on the war, on gun control, or education, than perhaps can a man. Isn't a mother going to be against wholesale bombing, for tougher gun control, for better schools? However, you must also guard against being pushed into unreasonable or irresponsible extreme positions by your erstwhile supporters. I was the only major candidate running in Denver last fall who would attend and speak at an abortion panel hearing held at a local college. But I was criticized by some women there when I tried to emphasize my support for birth control and family planning programs, rather than an "abortion on demand" policy. It is all too easy to become a "Kamikaze candidate"—crashing and burning on one or two emotionally packed issues.

So, it can be done. Women can run. And win. "You can do it!" I hope there will be questions later, and I look forward to talking with many of you individually later on today. Thank you.

MALAISE OF THE SPIRIT

RECONCILIATION AND PEACE [1]

Mark O. Hatfield [2]

A dramatic moment occurred on February 1, 1972, at the Annual National Prayer Breakfast, held in the International Ballroom of the Washington Hilton Hotel. Mark O. Hatfield, Republican senator from Oregon, a devout Baptist and longtime member of the Senate prayer group, bowing to his conscience, told the three thousand leaders attending: "Today our prayers must begin with repentance. Individually we must seek forgiveness for the exile of love from hearts. And corporately as a people we must turn in repentance from the sin that has scarred our national soul."

Because of his long outspoken opposition to the Vietnam war, his listeners knew that he referred to American involvement in Southeast Asia. What added to the drama was the presence of President Nixon at the breakfast. Among the other listeners were hawkish congressmen, Air Force and Army generals, Navy admirals, and representatives from 120 other nations. The New York *Times* (February 2, 1973) reported that Hatfield received "both sustained and energetic" applause. When he spoke a few minutes later, President Nixon made no mention of what Senator Hatfield had said.

Other speakers included Representative Albert H. Quie, (Republican, Minnesota), Representative John T. Myers, (Republican, Indiana), Arthur F. Burns, chairman of the Federal Reserve Board, Harry A. Blackmun, associate justice of the Supreme Court who read the Scriptures, and Rev. Billy Graham, who gave the closing prayer.

No one, of course, questioned the sincerity and good purpose of the Oregon senator, who was known as a good churchman. For a week, he confessed, he had struggled "between propriety and conscience." He later stated that he thought that such services as the prayer breakfast "seem to be using God and what should be a deeply spiritual experience to merely create some surface justi-

[1] Speech delivered at the Annual Prayer Breakfast, Washington, D.C., February 1, 1973. Quoted by permission.

[2] For biographical note, see Appendix.

fication for policies that have already been enacted." Many who heard the brief speech were moved to search their own inner feelings about the war and its results. Senator Hatfield opened his presentation with a statement calling for a moment of silent prayer for Senator John Stennis (Democrat, Mississippi), who had suffered grevious gun wounds from three assailants. After this moment of prayer, Hatfield began the main part of his speech. The two parts were not logically connected, but the first set the mood for Hatfield's main presentation.

Mr. President, Mrs. Nixon, ladies and gentlemen: As I see this audience this morning, we in the Senate Prayer Breakfast who meet on Wednesday of each week cannot help but be especially mindful of our leader of that breakfast group who has, over the years, provided the continuity, provided us with the stimulus to make our attendance known. And I see in this audience a great resource to try to bridge into what oftentimes is thought of as a withdrawn, rather exclusive group that meets on Wednesday morning. May I break tradition and ask each of you in your own way and in conformity with your own faith to mobilize together in this great room today the power of prayer on behalf of John Stennis, our leader, and do this silently for just a few seconds.

[Silence]

Thank you.

My brothers and sisters, as we gather at this prayer breakfast, let us beware of the real danger of misplaced allegiance, if not outright idolatry, to the extent that we failed to distinguish between the god of civil religion and the God who reveals himself in the Scriptures and Jesus Christ. For if we as leaders appeal to the god of civil religion, then our faith is in a small and exclusive deity, a loyal spiritual adviser to power and prestige, the defender of only the American nation, the object of a national folk religion devoid of moral content.

But if we pray to the Biblical God of justice and righteousness, we fall under God's judgment for calling upon His name but failing to obey His commandments. Our Lord

Jesus Christ confronts false petitioners who disobey the word of God when He said, "Why do you call me Lord, Lord, and do not the things I say?"

God tells us that acceptable worship and obedience are expressed by specific acts of love and justice. As Isaiah taught us, "Is not this what I require of you to loose the fetters of injustice, to snap every yoke and set free those who have been crushed? Is it not sharing your food with the hungry, taking the homeless poor into your house, clothing the naked when you meet them, and never evading the duty to kinsfolk?"

We sit here today as the wealthy and the powerful. But let us not forget that those who truly follow Christ will more often find themselves not with comfortable majorities, but with miserable minorities.

Today our prayers must begin with repentance. Individually, we must seek forgiveness for the exile of love from our hearts. And corporately as a people, we must turn in repentance from the sin that has scarred our national soul. "If My people shall humble themselves and pray and seek My face and turn from their wicked ways, then will I forgive their sins and heal their lands."

We need a confessing church, a body of people who confess Jesus as Lord and are prepared to live by their confession. Lives lived under the Lordship of Jesus Christ at this point in our history may well put us at odds with values of our society, abuses of political power, and cultural conformity of our church. We need those who seek to honor the claims of discipleship, those who live in active obedience to the call, "Do not be conformed to this world, but be transformed by the renewing of your minds." We must continually be transformed by Jesus Christ and take His command seriously.

Let us be Christ's messengers of reconciliation and peace. Then we can soothe the wounds of war and renew the face of the earth and all mankind.

Thank you.

IS THOMAS JEFFERSON RELEVANT? [3]

WILLIAM PEDEN [4]

The celebration of the birth of Thomas Jefferson has long been a tradition. His birthday, April 13, is a legal holiday in Alabama and Missouri. The University of Missouri at Columbia annually commemorates Jefferson's birth (the university was the first institution of its kind to be established in the Louisiana Purchase).

Typical of the interest in Jefferson elsewhere was the move of the National Endowment for the Humanities to launch the Jefferson Lecture in Humanities, with Lionel Trilling, the eminent scholar, critic, and teacher, as the first lecturer. Trilling was selected from among more than two hundred nominations by twenty-six distinguished private citizens appointed by the President. He spoke on the subject "Mind and the Modern World," on April 26, 1972, over National Public Radio from Washington, D.C.

The speaker on April 13, 1972, at the University of Missouri, was William Peden, professor of English, who has long studied the career of the famous Virginian. Professor Loren Reid of the Department of Speech and Dramatic Arts introduced the speaker. Included below are Reid's remarks, which in themselves are worthy of study, for they demonstrate the qualities appropriate for a formal introduction.

The Peden speech was carefully constructed. When the speaker suggested that Jefferson's vision of empire was not relevant today, he probably shocked some of his listeners, who came to hear praise of Jefferson; but Peden hoped to stir his listeners to think deeply and soberly. Indeed, the speech seemed pessimistic until Peden skillfully drew an analogy between the restoration of Monticello and the possibility of "something larger and better" for the future.

The speaker was introduced by Professor Loren Reid:

> For many years, faculty and students on the campus of the University of Missouri-Columbia have gathered on

[3] Address delivered on the campus of the University of Missouri-Columbia, April 13, 1972. Permission to be published granted by Loren Reid and William Peden.

[4] For biographical note, see Appendix.

Thomas Jefferson's birthday to pay tribute to the many aspects of his genius. Since this institution was the first university established on Mr. Jefferson's Louisiana Purchase, and since the original tombstone from his grave stands prominently on the campus, a ceremony at this time and place has always seemed eminently proper.

Originally the Jefferson Day speaker was chosen informally, from members of the University family whose intellectual interests stamped them as Jeffersonian. Our speaker today years ago gave an address under these informal auspices.

Now the University administers a special award, the income of a gift of $10,000 from the Earl McConnell Foundation, to be presented each year to someone whose character and influence exemplify the Jeffersonian ideal. The honoree is selected by a four-campus committee, which solicits nominations from each campus. As representative of the Columbia campus, I can testify that the committee received the largest number of nominations ever, and that it screened them most carefully before arriving at its unanimous choice: Professor William H. Peden, of the Department of English, University of Missouri-Columbia.

I will suggest only briefly Dr. Peden's qualifications. He holds three degrees from the University of Virginia. In the field of creative writing he has won distinction both on and off our campus. For three years he was editor of *Story* magazine. He has been a Guggenheim fellow; a juror on the National Council on the Arts; a judge for the National Book awards. He has edited ten or a dozen collections of short stories. He has written numerous short stories, articles, and book reviews. He has written on aspects of the Jefferson bibliography, has edited an edition of *Notes on the State of Virginia,* has written an introduction to Jefferson's library catalogue, and has completed a novel, *Twilight at Monticello.* I am not attempting to give you a full list of his achievements, but just those I happen to recall. It is with pleasure that I present Dr. Peden, who will speak on "Is Jefferson Relevant?"

As most school children know (or, I think, used to know, at least in Virginia and Massachusetts) the two principal architects of the American Declaration of Independence died within a few hours of each other, precisely half a century after the signing of the Declaration of Independence. The last words of ancient John Adams, dying in Massachusetts on July 4, 1826, are said to have been "Thomas Jefferson still lives."

The statement is meaningful and to a degree prophetic. Mr. Jefferson, whose birthday we celebrate today and whose tombstone stands out there in Francis Quadrangle, defined the goals and articulated the optimistic and hopeful philosophy of the American dream of empire. This dream, summarized and over-simplified, is based on Faith. Or, if you prefer, on deeply held and strongly cherished beliefs:

Belief in progress
Belief in reason

Belief in education as a means of individual and societal salvation

Belief in the concept of government as the servant rather than the master of the individual

Belief in the concept of human perfectability

Belief—unbounded and unqualified—in America and its future.

Let me refresh our memories with a few very brief quotations from Mr. Jefferson's public and private papers over a period of quite a few years.

"Truth and reason are eternal. They have prevailed. And they will eternally prevail."

"Error . . . may be tolerated where reason is left free to combat it."

"Educate and inform the whole mass of the people. . . . They are the only sure reliance for the preservation of our liberty."

"Let us preach a campaign against ignorance."

"We are destined to be a barrier against the returns of ignorance and barbarism. Old Europe will have to lean on our shoulders, and to hobble along by our side . . . as best she can."

"What a colossus shall be . . . a rising nation, spread over a wide and fruitful land . . . advancing rapidly to destinies beyond the reach of mortal eye."

These are noble ideas, nobly uttered, and as I said before, prophetic, too. The Jefferson vision of empire—not uniquely his, to be sure, and not exclusively American, by any manner of means—produced one of the great civilizations of history. But is that vision relevant today?

I am afraid I must answer by saying No.

And is there about it the faded—if glorious—aura of a Camelot, Shangri-La, or Never-Never Land? A dream rather than a reality?

I am afraid I must respond by saying Yes.

If no nation in history has progressed as rapidly as ours in two centuries (a mere tick-tock in the history of mankind), it seems to me that on the other hand no nation has deteriorated as rapidly in one eighth of that time. Allow me, if I may, to indulge in a personal recollection which Professor Reid mentioned in his very gracious and generous introduction. On another April 13, twenty-five years ago, I was talking here about Thomas Jefferson. World War II had recently ended. The United Nations was being heralded as the most powerful instrument in history, hopefully presaging the long, long dream of world peace. The power and prestige of our country, both at home and abroad, were at their peak. We occupied a position to which only that of the British Empire a century ago could be compared—and you all know what has happened to *that* Empire in the twentieth century.

To compare that occasion in 1947 with ours in 1972 may seem churlish—indeed, ill-mannered at this time and on this occasion—but I must repeat what I just said: If no nation in history advanced as rapidly as we, none has deteriorated as rapidly. I hardly need run down the list of our defections and failures:

We have polluted our air, we have fouled our waters, we have bespoiled our land.

Our economic situation—think of that multibillion dollar national debt—seems on the brink of disintegration. So too do many of our social institutions, and the very fabric of our individual and group lives.

We are disliked or despised by our former allies, feared and hated by our enemies.

Perhaps worst of all, we have grown to distrust our own leaders in all areas of our national life, political, military, economic. How ironic Mr. Jefferson's brave words sound in a climate which forces us to be almost daily witness to what seem at worst deliberate lies on a grand scale, or at best conscious distortions of the truth; in which perjury, on a grand scale, has become a commonplace. One sad example out of many: one week ago on national television, prime time, the Vice President of our country could say: "the Vietnamese war may go down as the most moral act in American history."

In such a context I cannot say with John Adams that Thomas Jefferson still lives or that his ideas are relevant: Rather, as a mythical returnee from the age of Jefferson and Adams might say: "Your ideas are dead, Old Man. Your dreams have ended, your vision has faded away. Do not come back; rest oblivious and forgotten in your grave on the quiet hillside in Albemarle County."

Hopefully, however, that is a pessimistic over-reaction, or an over-simplification as, indeed, are the statements by Mr. Jefferson himself which I quoted earlier. They represent one aspect of Jefferson, the romantic intellectual, the idealistic visionary. Yet he was never *just* a visionary. This most complex and paradoxical man of our history possessed at the very center of his moral, ethical, and political being a hard unyielding core of skepticism and doubt. If this ultimately unbridgeable gulf between the practical and the ideal is the fatal flaw in the Jeffersonian concept of empire, it is also, perhaps, the fatal flaw in our concept of our national destiny. Perhaps this can be suggested in terms of a metaphor or symbol or objective correlative: the plantation at Monticello.

Both as symbol and reality, Monticello is central to Jefferson in the same way, say, that the odes of Keats are central to an understanding of his life and achievement. There is no such thing, of course, as perfection in art; but at rare times, in rare individuals, a human being approximates the perfection which is inherent within a specific art form. In lyric poetry, for example, it seems to me that we find this in the "Ode to a Nightingale" or the "Ode on a Grecian Urn"; in music, in the last piano concertos of Mozart or the later quartets of Beethoven; in sculpture, in the "David" of Michelangelo; in architecture, Monticello, Mr. Jefferson's "own dear Monticello."

Jefferson designed and began Monticello in the early years of his adulthood, worked on it indefatigably throughout much of his long and busy career, and finally achieved in it what I think Aristotle meant by magnanimity or St. Thomas by radiance. That building, those grounds—a fusion of land and sky and the works of man—approximate a kind of order and ultimate harmony which suggest something far beyond observable reality. And yet, as you probably know, even during its creator's lifetime not only did the physical building decay, but it occasionally housed anguish and despair and violence. It suggests nobility; at the same time within its walls there were some deeds ignobly and terribly done. And after Mr. Jefferson's death the mansion and the grounds, in effect, commenced to return to their native elements.

Bats, it has been said, made their nests in the Dome Room, where Jefferson's favorite daughter and his son-in-law Thomas Mann Randolph had reared their children. The spacious entry hall became a place where refuse was kept and where a caretaker's goats were bedded down.

It's a sad and disturbing picture, just as I think our national history is in many ways sad and disturbing. But it has a happy ending. The building and the grounds have been restored. They are *there* and hopefully they will be there for a long time, as may our nation and its place in a world in which order and reason still have meaning.

Hopefully, in William Faulkner's words—which sound to me very Jeffersonian—we may yet endure, we may even conquer. Only history will determine that. Only history will suggest whether that tombstone out there is just that and that alone: a weather-beaten, tourist-defaced piece of coarse stone symbolizing death. Or perhaps it may be a guidepost to something larger and better.

Only history, too, will judge whether these lines, written by Mr. Jefferson less than two weeks before he died, are rhetoric or perhaps reality.

All eyes [he wrote from Monticello] are opened, or opening, to the rights of man. The general spread of the light of science [by which Jefferson meant knowledge in general, not just a specific scientific endeavor] has already laid open to every view the palpable truth, that the mass of mankind has not been born with saddles on their backs, nor a favorite few booted and spurred, ready to ride them legitimately, by the grace of God. These are grounds of hope for others. For ourselves, let the annual return of this day forever refresh our recollections of these rights, and an undiminished devotion to them.

THE ERODING AUTHORITY [5]

Lewis F. Powell, Jr. [6]

On Sunday, August 13, 1973, Associate Supreme Court Justice Lewis F. Powell, Jr. presented the "lay sermon" at the prayer breakfast held at the ninety-fifth annual convention of the American Bar Association, at the San Francisco Hilton Hotel. He spoke to an audience of one thousand to thirteen hundred lawyers, judges, and their families. On this occasion, Justice Powell, the former ABA president (1964-65), gave his first major address since joining the Supreme Court in January 1972.

The speech was only one out of seven hundred delivered at the meeting that attracted about 7,500 lawyers from throughout the country. In press coverage Powell's remarks fared better than many of the other presentations. It received front-page attention in such newspapers as the San Francisco *Chronicle,* the Los Angeles *Times,* and the Cincinnati *Enquirer.* It was widely covered in other newspapers and stirred much favorable editorial comment from editors of the New Orleans *Times Picayune,* the Boston *Herald Traveler,* the Fort Worth *Star Telegram,* the Baltimore *Sun,* and the Philadelphia *Daily News.* Large portions of the speech were quoted in the New York *Times, U.S. News & World Report,* Philadelphia *Daily News,* and *Vital Speeches of the Day* (October 1, 1972).

The speech grew out of the "malaise of pessimism" that has influenced many speakers (see preceding speech by William Peden). Social and political changes have been difficult for many to accept, and even more difficult to accommodate. The spread of crime, the rebellion of the young, the increase in the use of drugs, the questioning of marriage and family life, permissive attitudes toward sex, and the abuse of the welfare system have resulted in dismay, confusion, and bewilderment.

Justice Powell, a former Richmond lawyer, referred directly to many of these problem areas. Reflecting the conservatism of much of the legal profession, he deplored the "universal war on authority," "the alienation of so many young people," and the threats to "old ethics and values." He did not mention what he

[5] Lay sermon delivered at the prayer breakfast, 95th annual convention of American Bar Association, San Francisco, August 13, 1972. Quoted by permission.

[6] For biographical note, see Appendix.

had encountered on the bench, but he was probably thinking about the difficulties of reaching rational decisions in cases resulting from upheavals in American society. He suggested that "persistent and often destructive self-criticism is . . . a cause" of the alienation and that "excessive self-flagellation can weaken—or even destroy—the ties that bind a people together." As a conservative, he argued for less destructive criticism, more understanding of problems, and greater faith in traditional values. In his conclusion, he made a plea for the virtues of duty, loyalty, work, and self-discipline, and for the affirmation of religion.

When President Jaworski invited me to give the "lay sermon," my initial reaction was negative. I have never addressed a religious gathering larger than a small teenage Sunday School class. Even the latter made me uneasy, as I have no competency to sermonize to others.

Your President assured me, however, that you would be a tolerant audience—expecting little and hoping only for brevity.

Lawyers and judges are most at home when they are talking about "rights." I was tempted to select a subject in this area, as safeguarding the values protected by the Bill of Rights remains the highest responsibility of our profession.

But there is reason for concern as to other values, once held high in our civilization. I will talk briefly about some of these—without attempting to say anything original or profound. At most, in the meditative atmosphere of a Prayer Breakfast, I will ask you to think with me about some of the relationships and concepts that tend to be denigrated in modern society.

In general, I have in mind those values the individual once gained from respect for authority and from responsible participation in a larger community life. Today, we are being cut adrift from the type of humanizing authority which in the past shaped the character of our people.

I am thinking, not of governmental authority, but rather the more personal forms we have known in the home, church, school and community. These personal authorities once gave direction to our lives; they were our reference points, the institutions and relationships which molded our characters.

We respected and grew to maturity with teachers, parents, neighbors, ministers and employers—each imparting their values to us. These relationships were something larger than ourselves, but never so large as to be remote impersonal or indifferent. We gained from them an inner strength, a sense of belonging as well as of responsibility to others.

This sense of belonging was portrayed nostalgically in the film *Fiddler on the Roof.* Those who saw it will remember the village of Anatevka in the last faint traces of sunset on Sabbath eve. There was the picture of Tevye, the father, blessing his family, close together around their wooden dining room table. They sang what must have been ancient Hebrew hymns, transmitted from family to family through untold generations. The feeling of individual serenity in the common bond of family life was complete.

Sadly, this is not the portrait of contemporary American life. The refuge we once found in family and other community relationships is a fading concept. We are all familiar with the causes, though we may differ in evaluating their influence. The shape and style of our lives have been revolutionized by changes beyond our control: by advances of science and technology, by mass communications, mass transportation and the bewildering problems of an urbanized society. Whatever the causes, many of the old ethics and values seem threatened by new ones.

A nationally syndicated columnist, Joseph Kraft, recently described the reorientation of values as a "nearly universal war on authority." He referred to many young people who

> . . . assert their values in ways that are not benign. They undermine the chief restraint on Western society—the restraint of conformity, which is another way of saying respect for other people and their values. They are subversive of parental and school au-

thority. And as their protests gain attention and concessions, other groups are encouraged to follow suit. [Washington *Post,* May 21, 1972]

One need not be this pessimistic to recognize a considerable truth in what Joe Kraft says. The overriding concern —not merely of youth but of large segments of our people—often seems to be a highly individualized self-interest. In the familiar phrase, everyone wants "to do his own thing." Or putting it differently, self assertion seems to be the modern aspiration: to be independent of—if not indeed to reject —the familiar disciplines of home, school, church and community.

The work ethic, in many ways the cornerstone of a viable society, is also scorned by many—by some who simply think society owes them a living, and by others who equate dedication to work with a materialism which they wish to repudiate.

Perhaps the primary belief of the New Ethic is that the individual owes little loyalty or obligation to the types of authority I have mentioned, or to their traditional values. Rather, one's chief allegiance is to his own conscience and his own desires.

We see manifestations of this unanchored individualism in the new mores of our time. We see it, for example, not merely in hostile attitudes toward existing institutions but in excessively tolerant views toward personal conduct: sexual morality, use of drugs, and disobedience of laws believed by the individual to be unjust. Even the concept of honor is now widely questioned.

This is no occasion for a parade of horrors. I will, however, cite two recent stories in the national press.

The first described the flourishing new business of producing college theses and term papers, available for sale to the thousands of students who practice cheating. The University of Wisconsin is reported to have withheld grades from some six hundred students suspected of submitting, as their own work, papers they had bought from commercial firms. Many colleges and schools have been forced to abandon any pretense of maintaining honor systems.

Another recent front-page story was headlined "Sex at Home for Young." It described the "changing concept of sexual morality," and addressed the question: "What happens when the liberated young return [home] for the weekend, with a friend of the opposite sex and expect to share the same bedroom?"

I do not pretend to know whether immorality today is more widespread than in some of the other more notably boisterous ages of the past. It is certainly more visible and openly tolerated. But whatever the facts may be, the greater concern must be with the impact upon the home. The relationships clustered around the home, between husband and wife and parents and children, are the most sacred of all human relationships.

Leaving random examples, and returning to the broader causes of the alienation of so many young people, I wonder if persistent and often destructive self-criticism is not a cause. It has become increasingly fashionable to question and attack the most basic elements of our society. It is said that religion is irrelevant, our democracy is a sham, the free enterprise system has failed, and that somehow America has become a wholly selfish, materialistic, racist society—with unworthy goals and warped priorities.

It is also persistently said—and this is directed to lawyers and judges—that our system of criminal justice is repressive. If these criticisms are accepted, there is little wonder that our institutions and inherited values are no longer respected.

We have always been prone to self-criticism. Certainly no thoughtful person would wish to mute the type of debate and dissent which have strengthened our democracy. No traditions are more firmly rooted, nor more essential to the ultimate preservation of our liberties, than the rights of speech, press and assembly protected by the First Amendment.

One might wish, however, for a somewhat better balance and for a higher level of responsibility in the criticism. America, its institutions, and the values of our people deserve a better billing than they often receive.

It may be that—in our concern with the present and our serious social problems—we are losing a proper perspective of history. History enables one to understand the importance of evolution; it balances the frustration of "how-far-we-have-to-go" with the satisfaction of "how-far-we-have-come." It teaches us tolerance for the human shortcomings and imperfections which are not uniquely of our generation, but of all time. Indeed, it immortalizes all of us in the sense that we are not seen solely as the product of the present day, but as links in an ageless chain of human struggle and progress.

We, as a people, are entitled to recall that the history of America is a proud and decent one. However slow and painful progress at times may seem, the consistent American vision is of a society in which all men—without regard to race, creed, belief or origin—can live in self-respect and pursue responsibly their own aspirations.

It is of course true that we have witnessed racial injustice in the past, as has every other country with significant racial diversity. But no one can fairly question the present national commitment to full equality and justice. Racial discrimination, by state action, is now proscribed by laws and court decisions which protect civil liberties perhaps more broadly than in any other country. But laws alone are not enough. Racial prejudice in the hearts of men cannot be legislated out of existence; it will pass only in time, and as human beings of all races learn in humility to respect each other—a process not furthered by recrimination or undue self-accusation.

The frequently made charge that criminal justice is unfair and repressive is another example of exaggerated self-criticism. Whatever may be said as to the past, the present dedication to fairness in criminal trials—in courts throughout America—cannot be doubted. Former California Chief Justice Roger J. Traynor, whose name will rank among the great American jurists of all time, has said: "It is irresponsible to echo such demagogic nonsense as the proposition that one group or another in this country cannot get a fair trial. . . . No country in the world has done more to insure fair trials."

It would be irrational to say that all of the criticisms of America and its institutions are unfounded. Yet, excessive self-flagellation can weaken—or even destroy—the ties that bind a people together. This, it seems to me, has been happening in this country. The time has come when thoughtful judgments as to our institutions, and our role in history, should be tempered by the wisdom and perspective of history. In the long view, America has been a remarkably responsible member of the society of nations. Our system of government and our institutions have forged a country which in many respects has been the envy of the world.

I have referred to our history because it is inseparable from the traditional values of our people. The revisionist concept of this history contributes to the eroding of these values and to the weakening of the authority of the institutions which sustain them—the home, church, school and community. I believe these institutions are irreplaceable.

And as to values, I was taught—and still believe—that a sense of *honor* is necessary to personal self-respect; that *duty,* recognizing an individual subordination to community welfare, is as important as rights; that *loyalty,* which is based on the trustworthiness of honorable men, is still a virtue; and that *work and self-discipline* are as essential to individual happiness as they are to a viable society. Indeed, I still believe in *patriotism*—not if it is limited to parades and flag-waving, but because worthy national goals and aspirations can be realized only through love of country and a desire to be a responsible citizen.

Finally, on this Sunday morning, I affirm my belief in the *worthiness of religion,* and of its indispensable role in the development of the human spirit.

And speaking of the spirit, I am afraid that this talk—which I will now end—has done little to uplift our spirits. Perhaps lay sermons are meant to be this way. In the brief time available I have accented negative rather than positive aspects of contemporary America. There is much that is positive and cause for optimism. The idealism, and genuine concern, of so many of the young afford real hope for the future.

And we must always remember that the values and institutions, which now seem endangered, have survived other periods of doubt and challenge. In the ebb and flow of history, I am confident that their intrinsic merit will again be reaffirmed.

"WE MUST RENEW OUR CONFIDENCE" [7]

CLARK M. CLIFFORD [8]

Many persons have commented on the malaise of the spirit that prevailed among citizens during the fall campaign. Godfrey Sperling, Jr., of *The Christian Science Monitor* (October 10, 1972) observed about workers that he interviewed outside the plant gates of a big steel company in Pittsburgh: "There was a note of hopelessness in what most of them were saying." Then he generalized about these attitudes: "I find this same malaise all across the land and among voters all across the ideological and political spectrum. Much of this despair stems from a general disenchantment with—and distrust of—government and those who govern at every level. The recent charges being made in the Watergate affair, the Soviet grain deal, and the ITT case have not helped to restore public confidence in their leaders."

It is striking that Clark Clifford directed his attention to the same theme—"the corrosive and widely prevalent malaise that affects our national spirit"—in an address presented at the annual dinner of the Jewish Community Relations Council, November 1, 1972, in the Warwick Hotel in Philadelphia. This council embraces thirty-seven Jewish organizations in metropolitan Philadelphia; these in turn represent more than five hundred religious and civic groups. The audience was composed of about three hundred community leaders.

As he explained in his introduction, he was speaking in behalf of former President Harry S. Truman, who was the recipient of the council's annual Jules Cohen Memorial Award of 1972 but who was unable to attend. The award was given in 1970 to Roy Wilkins, national director of the NAACP, and in 1971 to former Representative Emanuel Celler, then chairman of the Judiciary Committee of the House of Representatives.

The ties between Truman and Clifford dated back to the period of 1946 to 1950 when Clifford, recently separated from the Navy with the permanent rank of captain, served as a special counsel to the President. In this post Clifford conducted an in-

[7] Address delivered in behalf of Harry S. Truman at the annual dinner of the Jewish Community Relations Council, November 1, 1972, Philadelphia. Quoted by permission.

[8] For biographical note, see Appendix.

depth study preparatory to the unification of the armed services and was influential in the passage of the National Security Act of 1947 which established the Department of Defense. Later, Clifford had important assignments under Presidents Kennedy and Johnson, serving as Secretary of Defense in 1968 and 1969. In 1967, with General Maxwell Taylor, he visited a number of Southeast Asian and Pacific countries as the personal emissary of President Johnson.

The Philadelphia speech now seems poignant in light of the former President's death shortly thereafter, on December 26, 1972. The esteem in which Truman is held by Jewish people was evidenced in a eulogy delivered by Rabbi David Benent of Congregation Beth Jacob, December 3, 1972, at St. Joseph's Church, Lewiston, Maine. In his touching statement the rabbi said:

> Indeed, there is little doubt that Harry S. Truman was the most important American non-Jew in Judaism's contemporary history. Eleven minutes after the State of Israel was proclaimed by David Ben Gurion, on the fourteenth day of May in 1948, . . . Harry S. Truman personally ordered de facto recognition of the new State. Truman's action served immediate notice to the nations who stood with tanks on Israel's borders.
>
> Had Truman not taken the action he did Israel could have been destroyed within hours.

It is uniquely appropriate that in the "City of Brotherly Love" the annual Jules Cohen Memorial Award for 1972 should be given to a man who has made such a deep and lasting contribution to the dignity of the individual and to the brotherhood of man.

I am honored to be selected by former President Truman to receive this award in his behalf. He asks that I express to you his profound appreciation. He is deeply gratified with your recognition of his efforts to advance the cause of equal rights for all men.

I am sure you share with me a sense of pride in the accomplishments of the remarkable American to whom we pay tribute this evening. His life symbolizes those qualities that have made America great. He has helped us see more clearly, and more simply, that original sense of national purpose, and those guiding principles that form the basis of the American dream.

To those of us who worked with him so closely, and love him so deeply, there is the greatest satisfaction in knowing that, with each passing year, the respect and affection for him rises ever higher and higher, as his place in history as one of our most illustrious Presidents becomes firmer and firmer.

As President Truman looks at his country today, he must be sorely troubled. I know that I am. And because I believe it to be the transcendent problem confronting us at this time, I intend to direct my remarks toward the corrosive and widely prevalent malaise that afflicts our national spirit.

I was in Norway, on business, in May of this year. Our Government, in addition to increasing the bombing of North Vietnam, had just ordered the mining of the harbor of Haiphong.

A high Norwegian official, with whom I was conferring, was shocked by our Government's action. He made a comment which has remained prominently in my mind ever since. He said, "America seems to have lost its way."

I asked him what he meant. He said, "America has always stood for what was right, what was decent, what was high-minded. Many of us don't understand the picture we now see, of a country that seems confused and uncertain at home, and at the same time is blockading and bombing a small Southeast Asian nation back into rubble."

I found it hard to reply. I had no ready answer or explanation. I do not criticize my country's policies when I am away from it, so I let the conversation pass to other subjects.

But this man of Norway, an old and firm friend of our country, left me wondering anew about our national purpose and our national resolve. Why does this attitude prevail in so many parts of the world? What has happened to us, to set us adrift, or so it seems, confused and battered at home, still mired in a miserable and tragic war overseas?

The America that Harry Truman grew up in in the latter part of the nineteenth century, and the America that I grew up in a generation later in Saint Louis, have vanished in the frenetic urban society that exists today. Everyone knows that the world has changed more in the last few years than at any other time in history, and that the very rate of change is accelerating madly. All of you, living in America's fourth largest city, can trace for yourselves the physical changes in your own lives, and I suspect that many of you would join me in saying that while we may have gained in affluence, there is something seriously wrong with the quality of our lives.

Has this change also affected our hopes and our dreams? Think for a minute about what our country stood for:

We were to be the great haven for minorities and refugees from all over the world;

We were to dedicate ourselves to a dream and a promise, of equality and equal opportunity, of free education and complete personal and political freedom;

And abroad, we were to stand for the same things we stood for at home, openness, generosity, justice, equality and freedom.

To talk of such things in 1972 may seem naive and ingenuous to some of you, but we would do well to consider what our country's goals and aspirations have been. Of course, we have not achieved all our objectives, we have fallen short of them at home and abroad, but we have tried, and we have believed.

There was abroad in the land, as I recall from my own youth, a feeling about ourselves, that we would steadily forge ahead, that if we worked together, pulled together in a spirit of unity and understanding, we would make life better for everyone.

What's become of America? That is the question my Norwegian friend was asking, and that's the question that you men and women, who are here tonight, must consider.

Recently Fred Hechinger wrote in the New York *Times* that

> what the United States seems to lack today is any one large, vocal and powerful group whose self-interest also coincides with the principles that once kept the American dream alive. The American people seem to have become largely incapable of rousing themselves out of their debilitating self-satisfaction. The result is a paralysis of the spirit, entirely uncharacteristic of Americans during the previous stages of their history.

That is a harsh judgment. But, I am reluctantly and sadly forced to agree with it. At every level, from the highest in the land on down, the majority of Americans, as Mr. Hechinger says, have "accepted the unwritten rules of the game: Don't rock the boat as long as you get your cut."

The paralysis of will and the lack of concern for our fellow citizens seems to permeate every aspect of our life. At the political level, for example, Americans seem ready to accept as a part of life the most outrageous actions, corruption and political espionage at home, brutal and senseless war abroad. And at a personal level, people in urban societies seem ready to live within their own tiny boxes, oblivious to the needs of their neighbors. When, for example, the noted Columbia University professor, Wolfgang Friedman, who had fled Nazi Germany in the 1930s to find freedom here, was attacked and killed by some young thugs in New York, within a few blocks of the apartment where he had lived for years, no one came to his help—even though it is estimated that perhaps one hundred people may have seen him put up a valiant but losing struggle with his attackers.

Again, I ask, what has happened to us?

Have we lost our sense of indignation?

How can we tolerate such things in our lives—lawlessness and isolation in our cities; corruption and cynicism in high places; apathy and indifference to massive suffering overseas; bombing and napalm in Indochina?

Have we become too materialistic, too self-satisfied? Have we stopped striving for our goals?

Why are we not the people we used to be?

Certainly Vietnam has played a major part in the current malaise of the spirit which I have tried to describe. After each of the wars in which we have been engaged, I think there has been a general lessening of the idealistic spirit of America. This is understandable. We usually rallied around the flag, and fought for what we thought was a moral absolute and a national necessity. Then we won, and afterwards, in the inevitable period of letdown, we would discover that war was basically and intrinsically unfair: while some young men fought and died, other men, usually older, profited from the war. I think that such feelings, for instance, enveloped us after each of the two world wars.

But those wars were widely supported by Americans. Men who fought and died did so for a cause.

None of that is true today. How can anyone possibly believe in the war in Vietnam any more? Men are sent off to support a corrupt government and bomb other peoples. And we are told that the justification for their sacrifice is that it is necessary for "our national honor." Can we not see the sophistry in this position, when in fact our national honor is daily being soiled in the mud of Indochina.

If the negotiations now in progress finally result in a settlement and an end to the bloodshed—and I pray to God that they will—the damage that this war has done to our national spirit will not disappear. Even on the day the war ends, we will be living with its dreadful legacy. Long ago, the war in Vietnam spewed forth a poison through the bloodstream of our nation, and the poison is still spreading.

It has destroyed much of the confidence we had in our institutions, in our government, and in ourselves. When we needed unity, we got divisiveness; when we needed honesty, we got duplicity; when we needed candor, we got deception.

Let me quote for you the words of one of America's greatest independent observers of foreign affairs, Hamilton Fish Armstrong. Mr. Armstrong has just completed fifty consecutive years as editor of *Foreign Affairs* quarterly, and, on that anniversary, he looked back across the decades from his unique vantage point and wrote:

> Not since we withdrew into comfortable isolation in the 1920s has the prestige of the United States stood so low. . . . The war in Vietnam has been the longest and in some respects the most calamitous in our history. It has rent the American people apart, spiritually and politically. It is a war which has not been and could not be won, a war which was pushed from small beginnings to an appalling multitude of horrors, many of which we have become conscious of only by degrees. The methods we have used in fighting the war have scandalized and disgusted public opinion in almost all foreign countries.

And now the poison is spreading even farther. We are reading daily in the papers about such affairs as the Watergate scandal—an unprecedented effort, apparently, to subvert and harass the normal activity of one of our country's political parties. Are we seeing the methods which have failed us abroad so badly, now returning to our own capital to haunt us at home, to spread further dissension and division among us?

But something else disturbs me—why is there no huge public outcry? Why is there no righteous indignation? As Hugh Sidey and Lance Murrow wrote in *Time* magazine, "What baffles many people who have witnessed similar episodes is why the nation is not up in arms over what may be the first documented case of political espionage in our history. . . . Where is the visceral sense that some fundamental arrangement of the society, some deeper human contracts or standards have been abused?"

I have suggested earlier that perhaps we have lost that sense of indignation because in the wake of this dreadful war we have become numbed and weary, ready to accept the view that the world is intrinsically rotten, and that therefore we should forget the larger issues, forget the "other fellow," and worry only about oneself. It would appear also that the young of America, who so courageously and correctly led the effort, which was partially successful, to change the course of the war, have now decided to turn inward because they feel discouraged and disheartened. A lethargy seems to have settled over our young people. Ask them, or their parents, about the Watergate affair, and the answer generally is, "Why, that's just politics."

If that is the national attitude, then we are doomed. The Watergate is not politics as we have known it, and we must not permit ourselves to accept it as such. There is something deeply awry in one's failure to be indignant over a wrong that's done—merely because it was done to someone else.

I lost, you lost, the American people lost—when Professor Wolfgang Friedman was killed in New York. But when not even one person, out of a hundred, would come to his assistance, we lost even more. This is a dramatic illustration of what the poet had in mind when he said, "any man's death diminishes me, because I am involved in mankind; and therefore never send to know for whom the bell tolls; it tolls for thee."

As a nation, we have gone through other difficult periods in our history and have survived. This time, however, it is likely to be more difficult, because it is hard to come to grips with a problem that involves a sickness of the spirit. It can't be seen—it can't be diagrammed—it can only be felt.

And it is also clear to me that we will not be led from this morass—we will have to extricate ourselves. We must find the means within ourselves to rekindle the faith and hope that are so desperately needed.

Nothing is inevitable about the future. We can continue drifting as we are now, or we can take steps to recapture the spirit of our past—the spirit which shaped and created men like Harry Truman.

If we want to do that—and I believe that we must do it if we are to survive—it is precisely to men and women like you that we must turn. If we are to work our way out of the apathy and ambivalence into which we have sunk, it will depend on the number of our citizens who *understand* the problems we face, *accept* the desperate seriousness of them, and are willing to try to *educate* others about them.

If just occasional voices are raised, it won't be enough. We must build a groundswell—a groundswell of decency, and honor, and character and—yes—anger—a healthy anger—directed against those who would deprive us of our most sacred heritage.

A man is known by the enemies he makes. Let us make enemies of apathy and futility, of hopelessness and cynicism—and let us stop being tolerant of the cheap and the shoddy.

This effort will take time, and I am not at all sure of the result. History teaches us that those great nations of the past that have perished, usually have done so, not from outside assault, but from a dry rot within their own society. In our present swamp of indifference and myopia lie the seeds of our own destruction.

In getting started on the task that confronts us, the first requisite is for our people to rid themselves of the feeling—that what they do, doesn't matter. We hear, all too often, the complaint that the individual can do nothing to affect our country's policies—that the people are powerless against gigantic and unstoppable forces.

This is nonsense. This is our country. It doesn't belong to any one group or any one political party or any one ideology. It belongs to the people.

But in order for our people to control their own destiny, they have to get involved. So I urge each one of you to leave our meeting tonight with the determination to rededicate yourself to those ideals to which most of us merely pay lip service.

Begin at the local level. Voice your determination to others. Organize for specific local or national objectives. Use the media to present your views to a wider audience. The basic will still exists, if the thoughtful people of our nation will begin to accept the responsibility of leadership.

To succeed we must overcome the curious and haunting sense of fear that seems to be associated with the act of becoming involved.

I can close on no more appropriate note than to remind you of the ringing words of President Truman as he closed his eight years in office:

> To beat back fear, we must hold fast to our heritage as free men. We must renew our confidence in one another, our tolerance, our sense of being neighbors, fellow citizens.
>
> Our ultimate strength lies not alone in arms, but in the sense of moral values and moral truths that give meaning and vitality to the purposes of free people. These values are our faith, our inspiration, the source of our strength, and our indomitable determination.

Thank you, and good night.

THE SIXTIES: LYNDON BAINES JOHNSON REMEMBERED

EDUCATION [1]

JOHN W. GARDNER [2]

In May 1972, the Lyndon Baines Johnson Library, erected on the campus of the University of Texas in Austin, was dedicated as a place to house the papers of the Johnson Administration. In recognition of the release of the papers on education, the first set to be made available for study, the library and the University of Texas sponsored a symposium, December 11-12, 1972, on equal opportunity in the United States. When he issued the invitation, Harry Middleton, director of the library, stressed that the purpose of the meeting was "not to look back, but rather to look ahead to see what this nation should be doing to fulfill its commitments in the decade ahead." (*Congressional Record,* January 9, 1973, page S351)

Explaining the occasion, Dr. James P. Rhoads of the National Archives and Records Service of General Services Administration, said to those assembled:

> With the construction of the Johnson Library on this campus and the planning for the Kennedy Library to be housed at Harvard, a new precedent for presidential libraries has perhaps been established, namely, promoting education by locating the library in a university community. . . . I think that it is symbolic that this precedent should be inspired by Lyndon B. Johnson, the Education President. His Administration was responsible for the passage of sixty major education bills, a record unequaled in the annals of American history. For this reason, it is also fitting that the first papers opened in this library

[1] Copyright 1973 by the Board of Regents of The University of Texas at Austin. Reprinted from *Educating a Nation: The Changing American Commitment,* proceedings of the January 1972 Symposium on Education cosponsored by the Lyndon Baines Johnson Library and The University of Texas at Austin and published by the Lyndon B. Johnson School of Public Affairs, Drawer Y, University Station, Austin, Texas 78712.

[2] For biographical note, see Appendix.

> pertain to education. These manuscripts will be consulted for decades to come by those who want to understand America's efforts to provide educational opportunities for its people. . . . This material will assist scholars in the study of the past and will guide policymakers in the determination of the future.

The symposium brought together many distinguished speakers and panelists, interested in educational reform, some of whom had been associated earlier with the Johnson Administration. Speakers included John W. Gardner, secretary of the Department of Health, Education, and Welfare, 1965-1968, now chairman of Common Cause, a reformist lobby for better government and honesty in politics; Wilbur J. Cohen, former secretary of the Department of Health, Education, and Welfare, now dean of the School of Education of the University of Michigan; Sidney P. Marland, Jr., commissioner of Education, United States Department of Health, Education, and Welfare; William J. McGill, president of Columbia University; former Chief Justice Earl Warren; Vernon E. Jordan, Jr., director, National Urban League; former Vice President Hubert H. Humphrey, now senator from Minnesota; Roy Wilkins, executive director, NAACP; Robin M. Williams, Jr., professor of sociology, Cornell University; and Julian Bond, Georgia legislator.

On the second day, Lyndon B. Johnson in one of his rare appearances after leaving office delivered a twenty-minute talk. "Until we overcome unequal history, we cannot overcome unequal opportunity," he said. "But to be black in a white society is not to stand on equal and level ground. While the races may stand side by side, whites stand on history's mountain, and blacks stand in history's hollow. . . . . It is time we get down to the business of trying to stand black and white on level ground." It was during this talk that he paused to take medication to ease the pain around his heart, a sign that pointed to his death shortly thereafter.

A little later, when the integrationist and separatist blacks became involved in a vigorous dispute, Johnson again returned to the rostrum and spoke impromptu to mediate the quarrel. He urged the delegates to seek unity on goals and to work for possible results.

Each of the four sessions was followed by lively panel discussions, stemming from what the principal speakers had said. The planners of the symposium had drawn upon leaders in education and representatives of minority groups. Among those invited were Jacqueline Wexler, president of Hunter College; Frankie M. Freeman, member of the United States Commission on Civil Rights;

Richard Hatcher, mayor of Gary, Indiana; former United States Commissioners of Education Harold Howe II, now vice president of the division of education and research, Ford Foundation and Francis Keppel, now chairman of the board, General Learning Corporation; Roy Innis, national director, CORE; Walter E. Washington, mayor-commissioner of the District of Columbia; Representatives Henry B. Gonzales and Barbara Jordan of Texas and Yvonne Braithwaite Burke of California.

John W. Gardner provided an appropriate opening for the symposium on education. He emphasized that the "American commitment . . . is not to affluency, not to all the marvelously cushioned comforts of a well-fed nation, but the liberation of the human spirit, the release of human potential, the enhancement of individual dignity." He enumerated the laws on education passed by the Johnson Administration. His introduction, referring to Thomas Jefferson's writing of the Declaration of Independence, seems particularly well conceived to set the mood and theme of the conference.

Let me begin with a bit of history. The time is June 1776. The scene—a second-floor parlor in the brick house of a young German named Graff, at the southwest corner of Market and Seventh streets in Philadelphia. There, shortly after the eleventh of June, beginning perhaps on the very evening of the eleventh, the lodger who occupied the second floor of Graff's home began to draft one of the great documents in our history. The lodger was, of course, the tall, lean, thirty-three-year-old Virginian known as Thomas Jefferson. The document was, of course, the Declaration of Independence.

Jefferson said that he "turned to neither book nor pamphlet while writing" the Declaration. Beyond that, we know very little about the actual conditions of drafting. If I could talk with the shade of Jefferson, I would pass up a good many other interesting topics in order to question him about the drafting. I would question him particularly about the second and most famous sentence in the Declaration, the sentence that, as it stands in the final version, reads:

We hold these Truths to be self-evident, that all Men are created equal, that they are endowed by their Creator with certain unalienable Rights, that among these are Life, Liberty, and the Pursuit of Happiness.

Jefferson later emphasized that he was giving expression to widely held views, and indeed he was. The Declaration, he said, "was intended to be an expression of the American mind. . . ." We know he had grounds for that assertion. As Julian Boyd put it,

> The idea that men were born equal, that they were possessed of certain inherent and unalienable rights, that those rights included life, liberty, and the pursuit of happiness, that it was the duty of government to protect and preserve those rights, that the government which did not do so could be abolished—these were ideas familiar not only to . . . every pamphleteer, every lawyer, every minister of the gospel, but also to almost every American subject of George III in the epochal year 1776.

"We hold these Truths to be self-evident . . . ." True to our modern temper, we have dissected the sentence, debated it, and impugned it. I myself have questioned it, defended it, argued over it, and written about it. But the dignity of the sentence remains. To me nothing can detract from the significance for Americans of the moral strivings reflected in that sentence. It is the most seminal sentence in the history of American values.

But we must not let our admiration blind us to certain facts. After the great words were written, eighty-nine years passed before we abolished slavery in this land of the free. Another half century passed before we enacted effective legislation against child labor. It was not until 1954 that the Supreme Court ruled against segregation. Even today human potentialities are warped and stunted in our slums.

Recognizing all that, what should be our attitude toward the words of the Declaration? I have heard it argued that in the light of attitudes and practices then prevailing, the words were sheer hypocrisy, the kind of lofty sentiment man expresses but never lives by, and that for the sake of honesty, they might better not have been written. I take a very different view of the matter. I believe the later gains in human dignity would have come even more slowly if the Declaration had not stood as a reminder of what we should be striving for and had not yet achieved.

Before the Constitutional Convention in 1789, George Washington is said to have made the statement: "Let us raise a standard to which the wise and honest can repair. The event is in the hands of God." When I was a young man, that seemed to me—and it still seems to me—a noble proposal. But as a youth, I was also attracted by its seeming simplicity. Life had not yet revealed to me how difficult it is to raise any kind of standard, nor for that matter how hard it is to be wise and how very hard to be honest—hard all the days of our lives.

I believe that Jefferson erected such a standard when he inserted into our first national document a clear expression of what has proven to be the most enduring of American values. We have been faithful and faithless by turns to the ideals that he expressed. We have interpreted and reinterpreted his words. Our understanding of the values underlying them has evolved and deepened. We are still struggling to do justice to the vision, heartened by our successes, ashamed of many failures, and unable to predict what new moral insights of tomorrow will make present practice appear primitive. Perhaps that is a description of the reality surrounding all moral striving.

The story of our failures and partial successes in the 196 years since the Declaration is more than the story of the slow approach to an early goal. Not only is our practice becoming in some respects more compatible with the Declaration, but also our moral insight concerning the goal itself is in some respects deepening. We understand more now than we did then about the implications of those truths that were thought to be self-evident. One of the things we know now is that there are other and perhaps more stubborn obstacles to individual fulfillment than the political tyranny and oppression that preoccupied the Founding Fathers—obstacles such as poverty, ignorance, disease, discrimination, and mental or physical illness or incapacity. These cannot be removed merely by assertion of unalienable rights, nor even by legally certified freedoms. The most exciting declaration of *our* generation is the assertion that we must attack *all* of these obstacles.

I listed ignorance as one of the obstacles to individual fulfillment and that brings me to the subject of this ceremony: education. President Lyndon B. Johnson is the only President of the United States who has ever said that education is the first business of this Nation—and he believed it, and he acted upon his belief. During his Administration, expenditures for education more than tripled. I could fill the whole of this speech with no more than the simplest annotated listing of the programs launched. I could talk at length about the Elementary and Secondary Education Act, about the programs to strengthen higher education, about the first national venture into noncommercial television, or about the assistance given to libraries and medical schools and vocational programs and rehabilitation. But the full record is available for all to read. I am convinced that in the decades to come, historians will look back to the 1960s as a moment of seminal change in American education, a moment of innovation, a time of significant beginnings.

Consider the matter of education for disadvantaged children. In the 1960s we undertook the first large-scale, intensive programs to improve the education of the disadvantaged. The efforts were massive, and they involved a great variety of approaches to the problem. We calculated that there were about fifteen million children living in poverty in the United States. The more closely we studied these children from our urban slums and rural depressed areas, the more clearly we saw the extraordinary difficulties they faced when they entered school. Unprepared socially and psychologically, discouraged almost before they began, they often dropped out as early as they could.

Many, many millions of children benefited from special projects under the Elementary and Secondary Education Act. They benefited from individualized instruction, from enriched summer programs, and from improved remedial programs. Many schools gave youngsters from poor homes a chance to learn and earn at the same time. Night classes were set up so that school dropouts could continue their education after work. New books, films, and training aids were made available. Counseling services were established and teacher aides were brought into the classroom so that teachers could devote more time to teaching.

Under the Economic Opportunity Act equally significant experimentation was underway, particularly, of course, the immensely important work in preschool education. There has been endless debate over the effectiveness of the Head Start program. But it had one undeniably good consequence, one irreversible consequence. We will never again assume, as our schools once officially assumed, that to assemble all children of an age group in school in their sixth year of life is necessarily to give them all an equal chance.

As we approached the problem of improving the education of the disadvantaged, most of us were acutely aware of the difficulties involved. Indeed the task was so difficult and the obstacles so discouraging that we sometimes felt very little sense of accomplishment. But we learned quite a few things:

1. We came to understand, as I have said, the importance of early childhood education, and we will not forget that lesson.

2. We came to understand the centrality of language handicaps in disadvantaged children.

3. We learned the importance of remedial education to these youngsters who fall progressively behind because of early handicaps.

4. We discovered the possibilities of individualized learning situations which permit slow learners to work at their

own pace at the same time that they enjoy participation in the class that includes more rapid learners.

5. We rediscovered the central importance of motivation and the necessity to alter certain kinds of self-image that lead to self-defeating behavior on the part of many disadvantaged children.

6. We explored many approaches to training for employability and the transition from school to work—better counseling, work-study, on-the-job training, and effective teamwork among the schools, the unions, and industry.

It appears to be the fashion now, at least in some circles, to be somewhat discouraged about the education of disadvantaged children. Many people have worked very hard on programs that have not fully succeeded. They have seen large sums of money spent without the clear, dramatic results for which they had hoped. They are still searching for answers.

But I cannot accept discouragement as a reasonable reaction. As little as fifteen years ago we were not even thinking about the problem. Almost everyone in the field of education assumed that somehow our democratic educational system automatically handed an equal opportunity to every school child in the first grade. If you cannot remember how complacent we were on that score, you have a very short memory. The education of the disadvantaged is a task of great complexity. What reason had we to expect easy answers? We have been at it a very short time. I sometimes think that we are long on good intentions and short on stamina.

Related to these efforts, and very close to my heart, were our efforts to provide equal opportunity to black children and to children of other minority groups. The Civil Rights Act of 1964 set the stage for that effort, and we took the first historic steps toward desegregation of the school system. I need not emphasize the enormous difficulties we experienced. One does no favor to the cause of equal opportunity by ignoring or suppressing evidence of real difficulties. But it would be wrong to write off the whole effort in a fit of pessimism as some are now inclined to do. In fact, it cannot be written off, no matter how anyone may feel at the moment. The movement toward justice for blacks and for other minority groups is an immensely powerful current in our national life. It cannot be stopped—not by the anger of its enemies, not by the mistakes of its friends. All who pursue the goal will not be infinitely wise in their strategies. They may have no ready answers for the dilemmas facing the movement at any given moment. They may make mistakes. But the movement will continue.

Let me mention one other field in which we made extraordinary steps forward—the education of handicapped children. We estimated that at least 10 percent of the school population, then roughly five million children, had handicaps severe enough to require special education. Of this number, we estimated that there were one quarter of a million children too ill or crippled to attend regular classes, needing to have schools brought physically within reach; more than two and one half million with sight, hearing, or speech handicaps requiring special educational services; more than a million and one half school-age, mentally retarded children; and almost a million emotionally disturbed children. The usual teaching methods do not always work with these children, but a very large percentage of them want to learn and can learn.

Nearly 90 percent of all the mentally retarded can learn to do productive work, and most can learn school subjects. In a four-year period, we approximately doubled the number of mentally retarded children in special education classes —from 393,000 to 677,000. We provided residential and community services to 400,000 more. At the same time we were learning more about mental retardation, learning how it can be treated, learning how it can be prevented. We encouraged more young people to enter careers of teaching, training, and caring for handicapped children. In a three-year period, we almost doubled the number of students in training in that subject at our colleges and universities. We steadily expanded the quality and quantity of these teacher-training programs.

There are those who said to me at the time, referring to handicapped children and, particularly, to mentally retarded children:

> Why spend scarce resources of energy, talent, and money on human beings who will probably never contribute significantly to the society, who will be marginal at best?

And I always gave two answers, the first a practical answer and the second, it seems to me, a conclusive one. The practical answer is that the result of the effort is the difference between a self-sufficient human being and one who is dependent, helpless, and a burden to himself and society. We can achieve the former and avoid the latter for most of these children. The conclusive answer is much briefer. Every individual is of value.

At the heart of our conviction as Americans is the belief that every individual should be enabled to grow to his full stature and be what he has it in him to be. Over the years we have become increasingly determined to fulfill that promise, and education offers the chief means of doing so. Most Americans had always believed in the ideal of individual fulfillment. What was new in the efforts of the 1960s was the breadth and penetration of the efforts that we made to make the ideal come to pass. Never before in our history had we worked so hard on so many fronts to open the avenues of opportunity. Never before, to cite one example, had we mounted a penetrating attack on hard-core poverty. Our concurrent attack on racial discrimination, another barrier to individual fulfillment, was incomparably more vigorous than any attempted previously. The same may be said of our efforts to cope with mental retardation, mental illness, physical incapacity, and so on. In fact, we launched the broadest possible attack on all the conditions that prevented individual fulfillment or stunted human growth.

I shall always be grateful to President Johnson for giving me the opportunity to serve as Secretary of Health, Education, and Welfare during some of those years. The job gave me a very special view of this Nation. I saw children being taught, sick people being cared for, the aged being helped, the disabled retrained; I saw health research going on; I saw the schools and colleges expanding, young men and women being prepared for careers in science and scholarship and the arts. I saw the people in and out of government who make that whole part of American society work—teachers, nurses, businessmen who serve on school boards, doctors, ministers, social workers, housewives who do volunteer work, college students who tutor children in the slums, and all those who give generously or raise money for good purposes.

Why do they do these things? Why do they do them with such conviction? To answer that is to say something about what I like to think of as the American commitment, which is not to affluence, not to all the marvelously cushioned comforts of a well-fed nation, but to the liberation of the human spirit, the release of human potential, the enhancement of individual dignity. Those are the great themes of our life as a people. Everything else is a means to those ends. Although some of our fellow citizens do not honor those ends, many others do. Many live by the American commitment and live to further that commitment. It can be honored only by deeds. The tasks involved in achieving the ideals that we profess are difficult, often painful. But if we say one thing and do another, then we are dealers in illusions and not a great people.

I saw people from every part of the Nation, in every walk of life, tackling the toughest problems of our national life. I worked with such people day in and day out. They came from all walks of life. Their occupational labels did not really matter. They constitute the brotherhood—and sisterhood—of those who care enough about the American commitment to do something about it. It is an army without banners and its campaigns are not reported on the front page—but it marches.

Every time a teacher strives to give honest, individual attention to some child, she is advancing the cause. Every time an employer seeks to create the working environment in which individual employees can flourish and grow, he is helping. Every time a mother provides the special combination of love and instruction that makes for early intellectual growth, she is doing her bit. Every time a citizen works through a civic organization to create a government more responsive to individuals, he is contributing. In short, anyone can contribute, and I must say I count the contribution as a measure of the men and women I meet. I do not want to know what their religion is or what political party they belong to or what philosophy they profess. I just want to know what they have done lately about the basic American commitment. The commitment is deeper than political parties. It has to do with a powerful current that runs beneath the surface of American life down through the years and the decades and the generations—and we must keep it running strong.

Some believe that in the interest of humanitarianism we should weave a vast cocoon around everyone in the society so that everyone will be safe and secure and problems will disappear. But that is impossible. We cannot make everyone safe and secure. We cannot hope for a world without problems. What we can hope for is a society in which every individual has a chance and no individual is irreparably damaged by circumstances that can be prevented.

Every individual is of value. That defines the purpose of our efforts. That is the purpose of all our trials and errors, all our seeking and finding. We must enhance the individual human being. That is easy to lose sight of, especially when we are talking about huge government programs, but their only legitimate purpose is to create the conditions in which individual lives may be lived humanely.

What I am saying, then, is first, that there is contained in this great Library a record of some of the most exciting years in the history of American education; and second, that the story told therein is at the very heart of what this Nation is about.

In closing, I want to pay tribute to the important leadership supplied by Francis Keppel and Harold Howe, who served as Commissioners of Education during my years as Secretary. And I want again to extend my thanks to President Lyndon B. Johnson, whose powerful convictions made all of this possible.

EULOGY OF LYNDON BAINES JOHNSON [3]

DEAN RUSK [4]

On January 22, 1973, Lyndon Baines Johnson, the thirty-sixth President of the United States, had a fatal heart attack. The following day, President Richard M. Nixon paid tribute to his predecessor in a message announcing the ending of the Vietnam war:

> Just yesterday, a great American, who once occupied this office, died. In his life President Johnson endured the vilification of those who sought to portray him as a man of war. But there was nothing he cared about more deeply than achieving a lasting peace in the world.
>
> I remember the last time I talked with him. . . . He spoke then of his concern with bringing peace, with making it the right kind of peace, and I was grateful that he once again expressed his support for my efforts to gain such a peace. No one would have welcomed this peace more than he.

The three-day funeral began at the Lyndon Baines Johnson Library at the University of Texas where Mrs. Johnson and her two daughters, near the catafalque received dignitaries and friends who came to express their sympathy to the family. Next followed a state funeral in Washington. As is traditional, the coffin, mounted on a horse-drawn caisson, was carried through crowded streets to the Capitol Rotunda, where it rested for seventeen hours.

Memorial services honoring the former President were held in the Rotunda of the Capitol, at the National City Christian Church in Washington, and finally at the graveside on the Johnson ranch. Speeches were delivered in the House of Representatives and the Senate, at the University of Texas, and in the Texas legislature (see *Congressional Record,* February 6, 1972, pages H731-H779). Speakers recalled their memories of Lyndon Johnson at his best. Many speeches, filled with superlatives, were elaborate and strained for eloquence. Perhaps Richard Boeth of *Newsweek* (February 5, 1973) best explained why many of these speeches fell short of capturing the spirit of Johnson: "From the little bar-

[3] Eulogy delivered in the Rotunda of the Capitol, Washington, D.C. at a memorial service, January 24, 1973. Quoted by permission.

[4] For biographical note, see Appendix.

bershop in Johnson City to the Rotunda of the Capitol, men and women who had known him spoke flounderingly of him as 'a giant,' 'outsized,' 'larger than life'—inadequate terminology trying to capture the sense that LBJ wanted, acted, felt, succeeded and failed on a scale that most men could not even imagine." The eulogy presented here was one which Dean Rusk, Johnson's Secretary of State, delivered in the Rotunda of the Capitol, January 24, 1973.

As a speech of praise, the eulogy attempts to emphasize virtues and minimize vices. It is a type of public address that requires careful construction and polished language. In recent years, Adlai Stevenson excelled with his superb eulogies of Winston Churchill (REPRESENTATIVE AMERICAN SPEECHES: 1964-1965 pages 103-107), Eleanor Roosevelt (REPRESENTATIVE AMERICAN SPEECHES: 1962-1963, pages 178-183), and John F. Kennedy (REPRESENTATIVE AMERICAN SPEECHES: 1963-1964, pages 31-33).

Dean Rusk, a long-time associate of Lyndon Johnson, was a good choice as eulogist. Avoiding overelaborate or flowery language, Rusk cast his remarks in plain style. Woven into his presentation were many suggestions of Johnson's virtues: "his deep compassion for his fellow men," "most demanding upon himself," "a powerful intellect went directly to the heart of the issues under discussion," "putting himself in the other fellow's shoes," and "a personal code . . . which did not permit him . . . to engage in personal vilification." Rusk skillfully focused upon Johnson's achievements in domestic affairs and avoided the controversial involvement in Vietnam. He also inserted a great number of specific details. The reader is likely to agree with Rusk that "a few strokes of the brush cannot portray this man. . . ." Those interested in reading a variation of the eulogy should see "Some Friends of President Johnson," broadcast over CBS Network, January 24, 1973 (*Congressional Record,* January 31, 1973, page S 1673).

A home on the bank of the Pedernales in the beautiful hill country of Texas, surrounded by his beloved family and the friends with whom he so fully shared his warm and generous spirit.

A home in this place where we are gathered today, in the Congress, which was his life for so long, filled with friendships enlivened by that political debate which is the lifeblood of a free society, but friendships cemented by the common task of insuring that the public business somehow would go forward at the end of the day.

A home for more than five years at the summit of responsibility, of responsibility and not necessarily of power—for he, as other Presidents, understood that many expectations and demands were addressed to him which were beyond his constitutional reach or, indeed, beyond the reach of our nation in a world community where we might persuade but cannot command. These were years of awesome burdens, but burdens lightened by the fine intelligence and the natural grace and the personal devotion of the First Lady who was always at his side.

And now he returns to the Pedernales to a home among the immortals, that goodly company of men and women whom we shall forever cherish because they were concerned about those matters which barred the path to our becoming what we have in us to become. More than a thousand years ago, in a simpler and more robust age, perhaps we might have known him as Lyndon the Liberator, for he was determined to free our people in body, mind and spirit.

A few strokes of the brush cannot portray this man to whom we offer our affection and respect today. As for me, I would begin with his deep compassion for his fellowman, a compassion which was shared by the Congress and resulted in the most extraordinary legislative season in our history.

Who can forget that remarkable evening of March 15, 1965, when President Johnson addressed a joint session of Congress on voting rights and other civil rights? It was perhaps his finest single message.

You will remember that, after recalling his days as a teacher of poor Mexican-American children back in 1928, he said, "It never even occurred to me in my fondest dreams that I might have the chance to help the sons and daughters of those students and to help people like them all over the country."

And then, with eyes which bored into the conscience of all who heard him, he said, "But now I do have that chance, and I'll let you in on a secret—I mean to use it. And I hope you will use it with me."

And then he went on to disclose in a very frank way what some of his deepest hopes were. Congressman Pickle has already quoted those hopes. One may give these ideas any name or epithet one might choose. They did not evolve out of some empty intellectual exercise. They were not the product of shrewd political calculation. His colleagues knew them as a volcanic eruption from the innermost being of his soul when the responsibility for leadership finally became his own.

Many have said that Lyndon Johnson was demanding upon his colleagues and personal staff. Indeed he was. And demanding upon the Congress and the American people and many a foreign leader as well. But he was most demanding upon himself and stubbornly resisted the admonitions of his associates to slow down. There was so much to do, and there was so little time in which to get it done.

President Johnson sometimes deprecated his own background in foreign affairs. Actually he brought great talents and a rich experience to this aspect of the Presidency in November 1963. As Senate Majority Leader throughout much of the Eisenhower years, he was necessarily and deeply involved in the widest range of legislation affecting foreign and defense policy.

When he became Vice President, President Kennedy asked him frequently to make foreign visits and consult with foreign leaders on matters of major importance—not merely a tourist's visit.

He absorbed briefings in a most expert fashion, and with a powerful intellect went directly to the heart of the issues under discussion. And as many present know, he was always formidable in negotiation or persuasion.

He had a special ability, perhaps learned in the Senate, to begin his consideration of a problem by putting himself in the other fellow's shoes, in an attempt to understand which answers might be possible.

He had a personal code of relations among political leaders which did not permit him or his colleagues to engage in personal vilification aimed at foreign leaders, however deep the disagreement might appear to be.

Today's writers are inclined to discuss Lyndon Johnson almost solely in terms of Vietnam, and such questions as whether he did too much or too little in that tragic struggle. The historian will take a broader view and weigh such things as the Consular and Civil Air Agreements with the Soviet Union, the Non-proliferation Treaty, our space treaties, his East-West trade bill, the beginnings of the SALT talks, and many other initiatives aimed at building the peace.

He had a very special and affectionate feeling for the nations of the western hemisphere. He used to say to us, "This hemisphere is where we live, this is our home, these are our neighbors. We must start with our own neighborhood."

Mr. President, last evening you made some moving remarks about President Johnson in your brief address to the American people. We congratulate you on the substance of that address and give you our best wishes for the weeks and months ahead. I mention two points which you made about Lyndon Johnson. That President Johnson was a man of peace and would have welcomed the peace which seems now to be opening up in Southeast Asia. How true. And he would, indeed, have joined you, Mr. President, in paying tribute to those millions of gallant and dedicated men in uniform whose service and sacrifice opened the way for the peace which is before us.

In his last State of the Union Message to the Congress, his final sentence was, "But I believe that at least it will be said that we tried." Ah, yes, he tried, with reckless disregard for his own life.

And then, in the final chapter of his book, when he was reflecting upon how it looked to him as he returned to that ranch which he loved so much, his final sentence was, "And I knew also that I had given it everything that was in me."

As time passes, the world will increasingly acknowledge that the "everything" that was in him was a very great deal, and that men and women all over the earth are forever in his debt.

AS THE DAYS DWINDLE DOWN [5]

LYNDON B. JOHNSON [6]

On September 16, 1972, at 8:00 P.M., former President Lyndon B. Johnson spoke to an audience of almost two thousand at the Temple, Texas, High School auditorium during ceremonies honoring the seventy-fifth anniversary of the Scott and White Memorial Hospital. This speech was Johnson's first since his heart attack in the spring. The appearance had special significance to him because in past years he had been a patient at the Clinic and had served as a trustee from 1950 to 1957. In spite of his recent illness, he appeared in good health and vigorous. Accompanied by his wife, he had come from his ranch at Stonewall by helicopter. (Temple, Texas, *Telegram,* September 17, 1972).

Explaining his acceptance, Johnson said that he "would like to get some things off my chest"—or, as he put it in his opening sentences, he wished "to share some personal thoughts . . . a concern for our country and its cause."

Not taking the occasion lightly, Lyndon Johnson gave considerable thought to the preparation of this speech. Consequently, he summoned Horace Busby, one of his former speech writers from Washington, to help crystallize his ideas. In an article following Johnson's death, Busby provided insight into how the speech was conceived and prepared.

> With some conspiracy and much complicity, various associates began working together after his spring heart attack, edging him back toward a more active public role. He continued to resist through the summer. At the start of September, however, he abruptly changed, for what reason I do not know. He accepted an invitation to speak at the Scott and White Clinic in Temple, Texas. From the ranch, he called me in Washington and asked if I could come down and work with him on what he wanted to say. . . . When I arrived at the ranch, he almost seemed to be waiting at the door. I was hardly inside before he

[5] Speech delivered on the seventy-fifth anniversary of the Scott and White Clinic, Temple, Texas, September 16, 1972. Quoted by permission. (The title used here headed a long excerpt published in the New York *Times,* September 21, 1972.)

[6] For biographical note, see Appendix.

picked up a favorite cap and headed outside, saying, "Come on, we need to take a long ride." For hours we rode together over the ranch. . . .

The ride continued through the morning and into early afternoon. Reluctantly, it appeared, he said he had to return to the house. "If I don't get my oxygen and my sleep," he explained, "I begin to feel it in my chest."

At his request, I followed him into the bedroom. He changed into pajamas, spent a few minutes adjusting the oxygen controls and finally slipped under the covers. Holding the oxygen mask in one hand, he began "dictating" what he wanted to say, gesturing as he did so with the other hand. . . .

He went on at exceptional length, stopping only when he felt, as he described it, "a little pinching" in his chest. Then he turned out the light and I went away to compose the first draft.

When I sat at the typewriter, I knew I had received two messages that morning—one was Lyndon Johnson's message about the country, the other was a distinct message about himself. . . .

It was late that night before Lyndon Johnson read the draft. He penciled through it extensively, far more than usual, and he read it aloud—to me, to Mrs. Johnson, to the ranch foreman.

When we were alone in the office, he read the first lines aloud for still another time.

"That's just right," he said. "That's just the way I wanted it."

On that December morning, three weeks ago, it was this speech—if not those lines—that was uppermost in his mind.

"As I look back on it," he said, "I think it was that Temple speech that turned things around. I think the things needed to be said and you just wouldn't believe how kind people are in their letters about it." (Published in the Los Angeles *Times,* January 28, 1973 under the title " 'The Country Isn't Over The Hill' . . . Then LBJ Was Gone" by Horace Busby. Reprinted in the *Congressional Record,* February 6, 1973, pages H761-H762)

This speech suggests that Johnson and his speech writer knew how to put together an eloquent statement. The introduction established rapport with the immediate audience; the reference to "September Song" moved the speaker quickly into his subject —but it also seemed prophetic of his approaching death.

Unlike some of the other speeches in this volume—sad and foreboding—this speech is filled with hope for the future. In answer to those who speak of the "malaise of the spirit," Johnson addressed the following words:

> Faced with a task of such great dimensions, we have no time for melancholy. We have no cause for moroseness. We have work to be done—the greatest work any generation of Americans has ever faced. Believing that, I say—let's be on with our labors.

Whenever I am in the presence of so many doctors and nurses and technicians, I am somewhat more accustomed to being spoken to than in having much chance to speak myself. As a matter of fact, when that fine introduction was completed and I heard my name called, force of habit almost caused me to lean back in my chair, stick out my tongue and say, "Aah."

Needless to say, I am very grateful to your fellow practitioners who attend me, from time to time, for making it possible for me to keep this engagement today. It is an occasion I did not want to miss.

For almost as long as I can remember, "Scott and White" has been a name spoken with respect and appreciation among my neighbors and friends. The people of central Texas have always known that whatever their circumstances—through hard times or good times—Scott and White would never turn them from its doors if they or their loved ones were in need of care.

On that foundation, Scott and White has grown in strength and influence and standing. Today—after seventy-five years—this great healing institution enjoys deserved recognition as one of our nation's finest health resources.

I am sure all the other laymen present will join with me in congratulating and applauding all of you who are making Scott and White what it is in the world of American medicine.

If I may digress for a moment, I would like to express my personal pleasure for this opportunity to be again among old and good friends in this area—from Temple, Belton, Waco, Killeen and other places.

You have meant a great deal to me in times past, for there have been occasions in other years when I did not rank quite at the top of popularity among members of the medical profession. Texas doctors tended to place me just a few points below chiropractors and a notch or two above Internal Revenue in their admiration and affection. At such times, I was always grateful that these blacklands of Bell County—outside these grounds—faithfully produced our state's highest per acre yield of good Democratic votes.

I am not here, of course, to speak of political matters. I am retired—more or less—from that line of work. But, if I may, I would like to share some personal thoughts with you about a concern from which I shall never retire: that is a concern for our country and its cause.

With the coming of September each year, we are reminded, as the song says, that the days are dwindling down to a precious few. By the calendar, we know that soon the green leaves of summer will begin to brown; the chill winds of winter will begin to blow; and—before we are ready for the end to come—the year will be gone.

If we permit our thoughts to dwell upon this perspective, these days can become a melancholy season.

As it is with the calendar, so it sometimes seems to be with our country and our system. For there are those among us who would have us believe that America has come to its own September. That our days are dwindling down to a precious few. That the green leaves of our best season are turning brown and soon will be falling to the ground. That before long we will feel the first chill winds of a long American winter—and that our nation's span as mankind's "last best hope" will be done.

For those who preach this prophecy—and for those who believe it—this period of our affairs can only be a melancholy season. But it is to that mood—and to the perceptions which foster it—that I want to address my remarks today.

Over the course of a long, full and gratifying life, I have seen many Septembers and known many autumns. In public service—and in private life—I have experienced a full measure of unwelcome winters. Yet melancholy is not a mood which I have ever allowed to weigh for long upon my spirits.

I live—as I have always worked—by the faith that with each passing day, we are always approaching nearer to the beginning of a new springtime.

It is by that perspective I see our country now.

If I believe anything of this land—if I know anything of its people and their character—I believe and I know that we have not come to and are not approaching America's September.

On the contrary, it is my conviction—a conviction which deepens every day—that this land and its people are quickening with the new life and new potential of what will become the springtime of a new America.

I do not say this merely to offer reassurance in anxious times. Far from it, I intend what I say to be taken as a challenge—a challenge to every citizen of every age.

No nation can be more than the visions of its people. America cannot be more than we believe ourselves capable of becoming. Thus, we are directly challenged to choose between two very different perceptions of what we are and what we can make of America itself.

On the one hand, we can choose to guide our course by the light of the bright perceptions—of America the beautiful, America the just, America the land of the free and the home of the brave.

Or, on the other hand, we can choose to move toward the shadows of what some have called "the dark perception" —of America the unclean, America the unjust, America the unworthy.

For myself—as, I am sure, for many of you—there is no real choice. I want to open the soul of America to the warm sunlight of faith in itself, faith in the principles and precepts of its birth, faith in the promise and potential of its resources and skills and people. Yet I know that, in these times, this is not easy.

For too long, we have permitted the dark perception to pervade our midst. Day after day, month after month, the portrayal of America as unclean, unjust and unworthy has been ground into the consciousness of our people.

We no longer see the blooming flowers for we are searching for the litter. We no longer celebrate the many fresh triumphs of justice for we are lingering over the residue of yesterday's shortcomings. We no longer measure the miles we have come toward a more humane, civil and peaceful world for we are too busy calibrating the remaining inches of times we are trying to escape and leave behind.

This is our clear and present challenge.

When we permit these dark perceptions to dominate us, we are allowing our future to be shaped by visions that are small and mean and diminishing to our potential. We are, in simple terms, dooming those who come after us to know what could only be a second-rate America.

This is a future which I am unwilling to accept.

I have devoted my time on this earth to working toward the day when there would be no second-class citizenship in America, no second-quality opportunity, no second-hand justice at home, no second-place status in the world for our ideals and beliefs.

I do not intend now that second-rate visions shall set our course toward settling for a second-rate America.

That is why I speak as I do now.

All through the pages of history—and nowhere more than in the history of medicine—we read the heart-rending stories of those who set out in quest of great goals and discoveries, yet where they were almost to the edge of success, they hesitated—not knowing or understanding how near they were to their aims. Out of that moment of hesitation, all too often they lost forever their opportunity to succeed.

In many respects, that seems to me to be a pattern we ourselves are in danger of repeating.

Over all the years of our nation's existence, we have been setting goals for ourselves and striving tirelessly to reach them. Those goals have been both the slogans and the substance of national affairs for generation after generation.

> Full employment. Decent wages. Adequate housing.
>
> Education for everyone. Opportunity for all.
>
> Good health, good medical care, good hospitals for
>
> even the least among us.
>
> Above all, equal justice under the law for all our fellow men.

America's goals have been simple and basic.

They have permeated and motivated all our institutions —churches and schools and professions and labor unions and corporations and foundations—as well as our governments at every level.

All our American resources and strengths—private and public—have been committed to the effort and we have come very close to success.

Nowhere—over all the globe—have any people, under any other system, come nearer to fulfillment of such aspirations than have we under our system.

Yet, at the very moment we were near to realization, we have allowed our effort to go slack, our momentum to slow and we have entered a season of hesitation.

Why?

Basically, I believe, it is because we have not understood —and still do not fully comprehend—where we are or what we are about.

Let me illustrate with one example.

Since the early Presidency of Thomas Jefferson, this nation has been committed—as no other nation on earth—to education of all our children. We have valued the minds of our young people as America's richest resource and we have honored that value by dedicating much of our wealth to development of those minds. Our purpose has been not to provide education for education's sake, but to equip our young people to be agents of change—questioning the past, challenging the status quo, changing the prospects of the human condition.

In our own very recent times, this long-sustained national effort has come to fruition. Never before in any society have there been so many educated men and women—or so many young people enrolled in pursuit of education. Yet when we came face to face with young people who were questioning the past, who were challenging the status quo, who were working to change the prospects of the human condition—we have hesitated in doubt and sometimes in fear of the educated young.

Across the full breadth of our national efforts, I could repeat countless other parallels. Out of the very success of our system have come the qualms and doubts that contribute to the melancholy of this season.

Whatever may be your own perception of where we are and where we may be tending, let me say for myself that I see little today suggesting that our system is failing—but I see all too much which convincingly argues that by our doubts and hesitation we may be failing the promise and potential of our system.

Our forefathers—all those before us—set in motion a system which would achieve change. The fruits of their efforts—and of their visions—have ripened in our times. Old values, old standards and old meanings have yielded to change. So have the old arrangements and old relationships by which others lived. We have perceived all this as signals and symptoms of a world in collapse. And with that perception, we have become susceptible to any and all who suggest that for our system, the days are dwindling down to a precious few.

But I argue that this is not reality.

We are not living in times of collapse. The old is not coming down. Rather, the troubling and torment of these days stems from the new trying to rise into place.

With our nation's past efforts, with our long and faithfully kept commitments, with our infinite successes in so many fields, we have brought into being the materials, as it were, with which to construct a new America.

We are not caretakers of the past. We are contractors charged with the construction of tomorrow.

Faced with a task of such great dimensions, we have no time for melancholy. We have no cause for moroseness. We have work to be done—the greatest work any generation of Americans has ever faced. Believing that, I say—let's be on with our labors.

The foundations are already in place, solid and secure.

We have beneath us the sturdy footing of the Bill of Rights—and it does not need us to be tinkering or tampering with it.

We have supporting us the strength and compassion of our great religious and ethical heritage—and that heritage does not need us to be denying it.

We have working for us the many decades of toil and labor invested in this system by earlier generations—and that investment does not need us to squander it by refusing or failing to invest our own toil and labor today.

The essentials of a new America—a better America—are all on hand and within our reach. It is our destiny—and, I believe, our duty—to take up our appointed positions and commence the labors that will change what needs change among us.

Our real challenge lies not in suppressing change but in utilizing it to vitalize and energize our society. Change is not our enemy. On the contrary, this society has no deadlier danger than refusal to change.

This is what I believe our young Americans are trying—and have been trying—to communicate to us. With their fine young minds, fresh new learning and clear new vision, they are seeing many segments of our society as it needs to be seen and understood.

They are telling us that government must change, business must change, medicine must change, labor must change, law must change—change not to depart from our system's principles but change to honor and keep those principles in new times.

A society engaged in the tasks of change will not long linger at the feet of those who preach that its days are dwindling down to only a precious few. A society caught up in the toil and sweat—in the thrill and excitement—of its own confident visions will not be drawn into the melancholy of dark perceptions.

At the risk of repetition—but in an effort to assure there is no misunderstanding of my purpose—let me summarize my message to you this way:

> This nation came into being because people wanted change.
>
> We went through some dangerous periods, but we have emerged with the best system that men have devised on earth.
>
> We need not, and we must not, chip away at the granite foundations on which our system is built . . . the freedoms guaranteed in our constitution and the new opportunities achieved in our own time.
>
> But this is not to deny that the system itself needs improvements, to meet the demands of a new day.
>
> Change and improvement can and will come. But it must not and cannot be change built on an effort to depict us falsely as a selfish, decadent and greedy land. The most frightening thing that could happen to us

> today would be for us to close our eyes to new ideas, and close our ears to those—particularly the young, in whom we have invested so much hope and effort through the years of our existence—who are trying to tell us how they would go about perfecting the visions of America the beautiful, America the just, America the land of the free and home of the brave. At the same time, we must help them restore the reality of America the busy, America the active, America the land of the confident and the home of the courageous.

It is just such spirit that we honor on this occasion. It is by restoring that spirit to our lives and our nation's life we can honor our own trust as Americans.

MANAGEMENT OF NATURE

HUMANIZING THE EARTH [1]

RENÉ J. DUBOS [2]

René J. Dubos, distinguished professor emeritus of Rockefeller University in New York City, microbiologist, experimental pathologist, and author, addressed the 139th meeting of the American Association for the Advancement of Science, on December 29, 1972, at the Sheraton Park Hotel, Washington, D.C. The association is the largest federation of scientific organizations, as well as an association of more than 133,000 individual scientists. Speaking under the sponsorship of the Agricultural Research Service of the United States Department of Agriculture, Dubos delivered the B. Y. Morrison Memorial Lecture.

This lectureship was established to reach "a variety of audiences concerned with the environment," and "to recognize outstanding accomplishments in the science and practice of ornamental horticulture and other environic sciences . . . to encourage their wider application to improve the quality of living . . . and to stress the urgency of preserving and enhancing natural beauty of man's surroundings."

In a sense, this address is an answer to the emotionalism stirred up by more pessimistic contemporary environmentalists. From a lifetime of study, experimentation, and travel, the speaker gives the listener a new perspective on a subject frequently presented in a negative way. *Current Biography* (January 1973) says, "His foremost concern is the preservation of man's 'humanness' by using technological advances to promote rather than destroy an ecologically sound environment." Looking at the limitations of the law "nature knows best," he argues that "the wisdom of nature is often short-sighted" and that "man . . . has . . . succeeded in humanizing most of the earth's surface." Although he is well aware of the problems generated both by nature and by man, he concludes that "by using scientific knowledge and ecological wisdom

[1] B. Y. Morrison Memorial Lecture, sponsored by the Agricultural Research Service of the United States Department of Agriculture, delivered December 29, 1972, to the 139th meeting of the American Association for the Advancement of Science. Quoted by permission.

[2] For biographical note, see Appendix.

we can manage the earth so as to create environments which are ecologically stable, economically profitable, aesthetically rewarding, and favorable to the continued growth of civilization."

To learn more about the thinking of René Dubos, one can read his comments published regularly under the title "The Despairing Optimist," in *The American Scholar*; his numerous articles in *Audubon*, particularly "The Theology of the Earth" (July 1972) and "Conservation, Stewardship and The Human Spirit" (September 1972); and his latest book, a collection of essays entitled *A God Within* (Scribner, 1972).

How grey and drab, unappealing and unsignificant, our planet would be without the radiance of life. If it were not covered with living organisms the surface of the earth would resemble that of the moon. Its colorful and diversified appearance is largely the creation of microbes, plants, and animals which endlessly transform its inanimate rocks and gases into an immense variety of organic substances. Man augments still further this diversification by altering the physical characteristics of the land, changing the distribution of living things, and adding human order and fantasy to the ecological determinism of nature.

Many of man's interventions into nature have, of course, been catastrophic. History is replete with ecological disasters caused by agricultural and industrial mismanagement. The countries which were most flourishing in antiquity are now among the poorest in the world. Some of their most famous cities have been abandoned; lands which were once fertile are now barren deserts.

Disease, warfare, and civil strife have certainly played important roles in the collapse of ancient civilizations; but the primary cause was probably the damage caused to the quality of the soil and to water supplies by poor ecological practices. Similarly today, the environment is being spoiled in many parts of the world by agricultural misuse or overuse, by industrial poisoning, and of course by wars.

The primary purpose of the recent UN Conference on the Human Environment, held in Stockholm last June, was to formulate global approaches to the correction and prevention of the environmental defects resulting from man's mismanagement of the earth. I shall not discuss the technical aspects of these problems but rather shall try to look beyond them and present facts suggesting that man can actually improve on nature. In my opinion, the human use of natural resources and of technology is compatible with ecological health, and can indeed bring out potentialities of the earth which remain unexpressed in the state of wilderness.

The disastrous ecological consequences of many past and present human activities point to the need for greater knowledge and respect of natural laws. This view is succinctly expressed by Dr. Barry Commoner in his fourth law of ecology: "Nature knows best." I shall first discuss the limitations of this law.

When left undisturbed, all environments tend toward an equilibrium state, called the climax or mature state by ecologists. Under equilibrium conditions, the wastes of nature are constantly being recycled in the ecosystem, which becomes thereby more or less self-perpetuating. In a natural forest, for example, acorns fall to the ground and are eaten by squirrels, which in turn may be eaten by foxes or other predators; the dead leaves and branches, the excrements of animals, are utilized by microbes, which return their constituents to the soil in the form of humus and mineral nutrients. More vegetation grows out of the recycled materials, thus assuring the maintenance of the ecosystem.

When applied to such equilibrated systems, the phrase "Nature knows best" is justified, but is in fact little more than a tautology. As used in this phrase, the word *nature* simply denotes a state of affairs spontaneously brought about by evolutionary adaptation resulting from feedbacks which generate a coherent system. There are no problems in undisturbed nature; there are only solutions, precisely because the equilibrium state is an adaptive state. But in a given area, there is usually more than one possible equilibrium state, and there is no evidence that the *natural* solution is necessarily the best or the most interesting solution. In fact, it is likely as I shall illustrate later that the symbiotic interplay between man and nature can generate ecosystems more diversified and more interesting than those occurring in the state of wilderness.

What is surprising is not that natural environments are self-sustaining and generally appear efficient but, rather, that many of them constitute clumsy solutions to ecological problems. Many of these solutions appear inadequate, even where nature has not been disturbed by man or by cataclysms, and therefore could have been expected to reach the optimum ecological state.

That the wisdom of nature is often short-sighted is illustrated by the many disasters that repeatedly affect plants and animals in their undisturbed native habitats. The repeated population crashes among animal species such as lemmings, muskrats, or rabbits result from the defectiveness in the natural mechanisms which control population size. These crashes unquestionably constitute traumatic experiences for the animals, as indicated by the intense behavioral disturbances which often occur among them long before death. The crashes constitute, at best, clumsy ways of reestablishing an equilibrium between population size and local resources. Judging from the point of view of lemmings, muskrats, and rabbits—let alone human beings—only the most starry-eyed Panglossian optimist could claim that nature knows best how to achieve population control.

Most surprising is the fact that, even without environmental changes caused by human interference or accidental cataclysms, nature fails in many cases to complete the recycling processes which are considered the earmarks of ecological equilibrium. Examples of such failures are the accumulation of peat, coal, oil, shale, and other deposits of organic origin. These materials are largely derived from the bodies of plants and other living things that have become chemically stabilized after undergoing only partial decomposition. The very fact that they have accumulated in fantastic amounts implies that they have not been recycled. Paradoxically, man helps somewhat in the completion of the cycle when he burns peat, coal, or oil, because he thereby makes the carbon and minerals of these fuels once more available for plant growth. The trouble with this form of recycling is that the breakdown products of the fuels are so rapidly put back into circulation through air, water, and soil that they overload contemporary ecological systems.

The accumulation of guano provides another example of recycling failure on the part of nature. This material, now used as a fertilizer, consists of the excrements deposited by birds on certain islands and cliffs. For example, millions of sea birds use the Chincha Islands off the coast of Peru as a resting place and breeding ground; their droppings, accumulated through centuries or perhaps millenia, have formed layers of guano from 60 to 100 feet in thickness. Guano, being rich in nitrogen, phosphate, and potash, constitutes an ideal fertilizer, and its accumulation therefore represents a spectacular example of recycling failure. Here again, man completes the recycling process by collecting guano and transporting it to agricultural fields where it reenters the biological cycle in the form of plant nutrient.

Just as it is erroneous to claim that nature has no waste, so it is erroneous to claim that it has no junkyards. The science of paleontology is built from the wastes and artifacts casually abandoned by primitive man. Admittedly, the accumulation of solid wastes in technological societies is evidence of a massive failure of recycling for which man is responsible. But this ecological failure is the expression of behavioral characteristics that have always existed in human nature. Like the great apes, primitive man was wasteful and careless of his wastes, and we have remained so throughout history.

The solid waste problem has become grave in our times because we produce more wastes than in the past, and what we reject is commonly of a chemical composition not found in natural ecosystems. Nature does not know how to deal with situations that have no precedents in the evolutionary past. The solution to the problem of solid wastes, therefore, cannot be found in the ways of nature. It requires new technological methods and changes in the innate (natural!) behavior of man.

Hailstorms, droughts, hurricanes, earthquakes, volcanic eruptions are common enough to make it obvious that the natural world is not the best possible world; man is not responsible for these disasters, but he suffers from them as do other living things. Of greater interest, perhaps, is the fact that nature is incapable, by itself, of fully expressing the diversified potentialities of the Earth. Many richnesses of nature are brought to light only in the regions that have been humanized: agricultural lands, gardens, and parks have to be created and maintained by human toil.

Until man intervened, much of the earth was covered with forests and marshes. There was grandeur in this seemingly endless green mantle, but it was a monotonous grandeur chiefly derived from immensity and uniformity. The primeval forest almost concealed the underlying diversity of the earth. This diversity was revealed by man in the process of producing food and creating his civilizations. Since an extensive analysis of the creative transformations of the earth by man would be impossible here, I shall illustrate it with one single example, namely, that of the part of France where I was born and raised.

Before human occupation, the Île de France was a land without any notable characteristics. The hills have such low profiles that they would be of little interest without the venerable churches and clusters of houses that crown their summits. The rivers are sluggish and the ponds muddy, but their banks have been adapted to human use and their names have been celebrated so often in literature that they evoke the enchantment of peaceful rural scenes. The sky is rarely spectacular, but painters have created a rich spectrum of visual and emotional experiences from its soft luminosity.

Ever since the primeval forest was cleared by Neolithic settlers and medieval farmers, the province of the Île de France has retained a humanized charm which transcends its natural endowments. To this day, its land has remained very fertile, even though part of it has been in continuous use for more than two thousand years. Far from being exhausted by intensive agriculture over such long periods of time, the land still supports a large population and a great variety of human settlements.

What I have just stated about the Île de France is, of course, applicable to many other parts of the world. Ever since the beginning of the agricultural revolution during the Neolithic period, settlers and farmers have been engaged all over the world in a transformation of the wilderness. Their prodigious labors have progressively generated an astonishing diversity of man-made environments, which have constituted the settings for most of human life. A typical landscape consists of forested mountains and hills serving as a backdrop for pastures and arable lands, villages with their greens, their dwellings, their houses of worship, and their public buildings. People now refer to such a humanized landscape as "nature," even though most of its vegetation has been introduced by man and its environmental quality can be maintained only by individualized ecological management.

Just as nature has not been capable by itself of giving full expression to the potential diversity of our globe, likewise it is not capable of maintaining man-made environments in a healthy state. Now that so much of the world has been humanized, environmental health depends to a very large extent on human care. Forests must be managed, swampy areas which are under cultivation must continually be drained, the productivity of farmlands must be maintained by crop rotation, irrigation, fertilization, and destruction of weeds. From historical times, the Campagna Romana has been infested with mosquitoes and devastated by malaria every time men have lacked the stamina to control its marshes. Similarly, farmlands that have been economically productive and esthetically attractive for a thousand years are invaded by brush and weeds as soon as farmers neglect to cultivate them. The rapid degradation of abandoned gardens, farmlands, and pastures is evidence that humanized nature cannot long retain its quality without human care.

It is true that many ancient civilizations have ruined their environment and that a similar process is going on now in certain highly industrialized areas, but this is not inevitable. Intensive agriculture has been practiced for a thousand years in certain lands without decreasing their fertility or ruining their scenery. Man can create artificial environments from the wilderness and manage them in such a manner that they long remain ecologically stable, economically profitable, esthetically rewarding, and suited to his physical and mental health. The immense duration of certain man-made landscapes contributes a peculiar sense of tranquility to many parts of the Old World; it inspires confidence that mankind can act as steward of the earth for the sake of the future.

Lands could not remain fertile under intense cultivation unless managed according to sound ecological principles. In the past, these principles emerged empirically from practices that assured the maintenance of fairly high levels of humus in the soil. But scientific knowledge of soil composition and texture, of plant physiology, and of animal husbandry is providing a new basis for agricultural management. During the past century, the sound empirical practices of the past have been progressively replaced by more scientific ones, which include the use of artificial fertilizers and pesticides. Scientific agriculture has thus achieved enormous yields of plant and animal products. Furthermore, experimental studies have revealed that many types of lands can remain fertile for long periods of time without organic manure, provided they are continuously enriched with chemical fertilizers in amounts and compositions scientifically determined.

Efficiency, however, cannot be measured only in terms of agricultural yields. Another criterion is the amount of energy (measured in calories) required for the production of a given amount of food. And when scientific agriculture is judged on this basis its efficiency is often found to be very low. Paradoxical as this may sound, there are many situations in which the modern farmer spends more industrial calories than the food calories he recovers in the form of food. His caloric expenditure consists chiefly of gasoline for powering his equipment and of electricity for producing chemical fertilizers and pesticides—let alone the caloric input required to irrigate the land and to manufacture tractors, trucks, and the multifarious kinds of machines used in modern farming.

Needless to say, modern civilizations would be inconceivable if the energy (calories) now required by agriculture had to come from human muscles instead of from gasoline and electricity. But it is a fact, nevertheless, that if fossil fuels were to remain the most important source of power, the sheer size of the world population would make it impossible to continue for long the energy deficit spending on which agriculture depends in prosperous industrialized countries. And there would be no hope of extending these modern agricultural practices to the developing countries, which constitute the largest part of the world.

No matter how the situation is rationalized, the present practices of scientific agriculture are possible only as long as cheap sources of energy are available. After the world supplies of fossil fuels have been exhausted, the modern farmer, like the modern technologist, will become ineffective unless energy derived from nuclear reactions, geothermal sources or solar radiation can be supplied in immense amounts at low cost. Thus, the future of land management is intimately bound to the development of new sources of energy, as are all other aspects of human life.

Of the 70 to 100 billion people who have walked the surface of the earth since *Homo sapiens* acquired his biological identity, by very far the largest percentage have lived on the man-made lands that have been created since the agricultural revolution.

In every part of the world, the interplay between man and nature has commonly taken the form of a true symbiosis —namely a biological relationship which alters somewhat the two components of the symbiotic system in a way that is beneficial to both. Such transformations, achieved through symbiosis, account in large part for the immense diversity of places on earth and for the fitness between man and environment so commonly observed in areas that have been settled and have remained stable for long periods of time.

Furthermore, the reciprocal transformations of man and environment have generated a variety of situations, each with its own human and environmental characteristics. For example, the agricultural techniques, social policies, and behavioral patterns in the various islands of the South Pacific are determined not only by geologic and climatic factors but even more by the cultural attitudes of the early settlers —Polynesians, Melanesians, or Indonesians—and then later of the Western and Oriental people who colonized the islands. Cultural attitudes, more than natural conditions, are responsible for the profound differences between Fiji, Tahiti, and the Hawaiian islands. The Pacific Islands were initially settled by different groups of people and, in addition to these early human influences, they exhibit today the more recent influences respectively of their English, French, or American colonizers.

The shaping of nature by culture can be recognized in many other parts of the world. As the process of humanization of the earth continues, however, it will increasingly be influenced by the fact that most of the globe will soon be completely occupied and utilized. This colonization process began, of course, long before the days of modern technology.

But the difference is that men now occupy and utilize all land areas except those that are too cold, too hot, too dry, too wet, too inaccessible or at too high an altitude for prolonged human habitation.

According to the United Nations Food and Agricultural Organization, practically all the best lands are already farmed; future agricultural developments are more likely to result from intensification of management than from expansion into marginal lands. There probably will be some increase in forest utilization but, otherwise, land use will soon be stabilized. In fact, expansion into new lands has already come to an end in most developed countries and is likely to be completed within a very few decades in the rest of the world. A recent FAO report states the probable final date as 1985.

The UN Conference on the Human Environment came therefore at a critical time in man's history. Now that the whole earth has been explored and occupied, the new problem is to manage its resources. Careful management need not mean stagnation. In many places, as already mentioned, the interplay between man and nature results in a creative symbiotic relationship that facilitates evolutionary changes. Man continuously tries to derive from nature new satisfactions that go beyond his elementary biological needs—and he thereby gives expression to some of nature's potentialities that would remain unrecognized without his efforts.

Man has now succeeded in humanizing most of the earth's surface but, paradoxically, he is developing simultaneously a cult for wilderness. After having been for so long frightened by the primeval forest, he has come to realize that its eerie light evokes in him a mood of wonder that cannot be experienced in an orchard or a garden. Likewise, he recognizes in the vastness of the ocean and in the endless ebb and flow of its waves a mystic quality not found in humanized environments. His response to the thunderous silence of deep canyons, the solitude of high mountains, the luminosity of the desert is the expression of an aspect of his fundamental being that is still in resonance with cosmic events.

As mentioned earlier, nature is not always a good guide for the manipulation of the forces that affect the daily life of man; but undisturbed Nature knows best—far better than ordinary human intelligence—how to make men aware of the cosmos and to create an atmosphere of harmony between him and the rest of creation.

Humanizing the earth thus implies much more than transforming the wilderness into agricultural lands, pleasure grounds, and healthy areas suitable for the growth of civilization. It also means preserving the kinds of wilderness where man can experience mysteries transcending his daily life, and also recapture direct awareness of the cosmic forces from which he emerged. It is obvious, however, that man spends his daily life not in the wilderness but in environments that he creates—in a man-made nature. Let me restate in conclusion my belief that by using scientific knowledge and ecological wisdom we can manage the earth so as to create environments which are ecologically stable, economically profitable, esthetically rewarding, and favorable to the continued growth of civilization.

VIEWS ON EDUCATION

PUBLIC EDUCATION FOR A HUMANE SOCIETY[1]

HAROLD HOWE II[2]

Vernon E. Jordan, Jr., executive director of the National Urban League, has referred to the fifties and sixties as "the Second Reconstruction," meaning that during those two decades the Federal courts and the Kennedy-Johnson administrations brought about and enforced much needed reform that offered hope to blacks for better schools, better housing, and fair employment. Contrasting those years with the present, Jordan expresses pessimism about the future. In a speech delivered at Howard University, June 3, 1972, Jordan said:

> Several major national issues offer ground for speculation that the Second Reconstruction is nearing its end. The failure to fully enforce the civil rights laws of the sixties is one. The ease with which the erstwhile friends of the civil rights movement have compromised on major legislation affecting black people is still another. The unwillingness of northern and western suburban communities to revise their zoning laws and to accept scattered-site public housing and housing for low- and moderate-income families is another major indication that civil rights is a popular issue only when it is limited to the Deep South.

It was this climate of doubt and uncertainty that influenced the National Conference of Christians and Jews to sponsor a symposium entitled "Quality Integrated Education," November 18-21, 1972, at the New York Hilton Hotel. Involved in the promotion and planning of this meeting were the twenty-three member groups, including associations as diverse as the American Association of School Administrators, American Jewish Congress, Future Homemakers of America, Girl Scouts of the USA, National Board YWCA, National Congress of Parents and Teachers, National Council of Negro Women, National Urban League, and Southern Christian Leadership Conference.

[1] Speech delivered at the National Conference of Christians and Jews, New York City, November 20, 1972. Quoted by permission.

[2] For biographical note, see Appendix.

The purposes of the meeting were stated as follows: to bring together people of varying opinions in order to clarify what quality and integration are in public education; to consider ways to move toward the achievement of quality and integration in education; to create a more effective awareness of human rights issues in public education; and to develop recommendations and guidelines for dealing with human rights issues in the public schools. The three hundred participants included government officials, businessmen, public school superintendents and principals, teachers, college professors, and young people.

The conference was organized around five work sessions with the participants divided into twelve discussion groups, each with assigned topics to consider. Harold Howe II, vice president for education and research of the Ford Foundation (formerly a teacher, school administrator, and United States commissioner of education), delivered what could be called a position paper for one of the sessions. His remarks served as impetus for the discussion which followed in the twelve panels.

The speech provides an excellent statement concerning the present challenges to integration. In the second half a solution is proposed. The idealism of the speaker is inspiring and deserves careful thought. The speech was well planned to forward the conference purpose: "to create a more effective awareness of human rights issues in public education."

It would be easy to use our time at this meeting reviewing the shortcomings of American society and its public and private leaders in moving toward the ideal of quality, integrated education. Indeed, I could work up quite a head of steam on this subject if called upon to do so. But surely the group assembled here needs no reminder that momentum has been lost in desegregating the schools, that partisan political advantage has superseded principle as the arbiter of racial discrimination, and that children continue to be victims of an adult society that imposes its prejudices on the next generation. The record on these matters is too clear to warrant debate, and we will use our time and our energies more effectively by asking, "What do we do now?"

Any response must start from a basic assumption about what matters. I submit that the only, acceptable, long-term goal for American society is a fully integrated social system without evidences of discrimination based on race, religion, sex, or national origin. Ten or fifteen years ago those who believed in such a goal were in the vanguard of social reform. Their views were widely accepted as the basis for changing public policy and for encouraging private action in reducing discrimination and enhancing the rights and opportunities of minorities. But now the picture is less clear. It is less clear for four reasons: first, minority-group persons (particularly blacks) have created their own separatist movements that threaten the spirit, if not the substance, of an integrated society; secondly, the lively researches of statistically-oriented social scientists have cast some shadows on conventional assumptions about the benefits of integration, particularly in the schools; third, there are still many people who feel or believe that an integrated society somehow threatens their jobs, property, or future security; and fourth, those of us who have provided leadership for the move toward an integrated society have not always been as wise as we might have.

It is not surprising that some blacks have since the mid-sixties rejected integration as the solution to anything and sought black identification, togetherness, and power. If those of us who are pushing so hard for integration had been sensitive enough, we would have been aware long before we were that it can be damaging to blacks both psychologically and economically. Early moves toward integration went too far in the direction of asking blacks and other minorities to join American society solely on white terms, to forget any pride or interest in their own heritage, or, if you will, to become white men.

Now we know that integration has to be a two-way street, that it is not just a simple matter of mixing people in some judicially or administratively determined proportion, that non-whites as well as whites must help to set the terms, and that these terms must include as a matter of dignity and right the opportunity for non-whites to lead and control some of the institutions in our pluralistic society. It is partly for this reason, for example, that I see the traditionally black colleges as significant. In a country where blacks don't run many essential social institutions, these colleges, that are numerically less significant every year in the education of blacks, have a special place in the resolution of "the American Dilemma." Of course, I hope and expect that they will become more integrated than they are, but it is important that the process will involve black leadership and initiatives.

Economically, blacks have suffered in school integration. Principals have lost their jobs, as have teachers, and blacks have, in general, lost out in the promotion and appointment processes of newly desegregated schools. This problem is starkly documented in a May 1972 report entitled "It's Not Over in the South" done by some of the organizations represented at this meeting. It is not surprising that facts like these have cooled some black ardor for integration.

It would be a mistake for me to take on the social science community in regard to the effects and usefulness of school integration as a means of improving the opportunities of minority-group persons in American society. I don't fully understand their calculations, and I can't claim to have reviewed their findings completely. But for what it's worth, I'll tell you in oversimplified form what I do get from reading Coleman, Mosteller and Moynihan, and Jencks:

1. They present no clear case for or against integration of the schools as an important social goal, although they suggest its limited usefulness as far as certain measurable outcomes of schooling are concerned.

2. They present a much clearer analysis of the pervasive effect of poverty on an individual's future opportunities, and they raise some serious questions about the capacity of current practices in schools to overcome the disadvantages of poverty. These analyses of the average results of current practices should not, however, be interpreted to mean that

a school is unable to improve a youngster's chances in life or that education does not pay off for the individual.

I do not believe that the work being done by these analysts of subtle cause-and-effect relationships in American society should be accepted by educational policy makers or by political figures as the major determinant for decisions on either school integration or educational expenditures. Their work is worthwhile because of its contribution to social science methodology and its future promise for illuminating our intractable social problems. But as far as school integration is concerned, it should not supersede the moral and legal basis on which we have determined that segregated education denies equal protection of the laws. Indeed, I am sure that the authors I have mentioned would agree with this point.

So in spite of problems and qualifications raised by blacks and by social scientists, I conclude that American society has no other choice for the future than to make integration work in its schools, housing, and other institutions. Basically, I think that this is the choice that will produce a humane society and allow a humane form of public education.

No declaration for integrated education is worth supporting without a recognition of the hazards and problems that accompany it. I'd like to divide these into two categories —those that are external to the individual school and those internal to it. In the first are all the familiar problems of bringing about pupil integration in a society that segregates its living patterns by both race and income groupings. Because I want to save most of my limited time on this occasion for the second category—problems internal to the school in providing a humane education—let me simply make five assertations about the first:

1. The degree to which integration of the schools is so dependent upon housing patterns that it becomes imprac-

tical has been exaggerated. With very minor increases in pupil transportation and with careful re-working of school attendance lines considerably more school integration can be achieved in both North and South. So called "massive busing" with all its emotional and political overtones is a red herring. There is no reality to it. The title of a recent pamphlet put out by the Legal Defense Fund has some basic truth, "It Ain't the Distance—It's the Niggers." Several states in the South have less busing after school desegregation because they are no longer carrying pupils long distances to segregated schools. At the same time, one must admit that there are some massive, central city examples of racial isolation that lie beyond the resources of the schools alone to correct.

2. The Supreme Court of the United States in its April 1971 decision written by Chief Justice Burger in the Charlotte, North Carolina, case [Charlotte-Mecklenberg Board of Education, et al. v. Swann] set forth a moderate and clear position regarding the constitutional rights of pupils to desegregated education and the obligations of school districts to provide it including, if necessary, the use of busing within limits. This unanimous decision of the Court is a landmark of good sense in a controversial area, and attempts to undercut it are ill advised.

3. Many of the initiatives that will be most valuable not only in bringing about integration but also in making it work will be state and local decisions—not rulings of the Supreme Court or legislation by the Congress. Current efforts at the Federal level to restrict the options of states and localities in using Federal funds to assist with school integration problems as locally planned also deny the essence of our Federal system and inhibit the opportunities of children. Such policies, in effect, say "No Federal money for brotherhood." In addition, this important area of local, voluntary action is significantly encouraged or discouraged by the tone of national leadership in racial issues.

4. Throughout the recent history of school desegregation efforts, whether legally required or not, those of us who have pushed for integration have shown an extraordinary insensitivity to the concerns of those groups known as "the ethnics" or sometimes as "the hardhats" in American society. Whether justified or not, these lower-middle-income Americans have had genuine fears that we have failed to appreciate and that we should not dismiss as being solely racist in nature. We are now living with the results of that failure. It would be unreasonable to expect blacks and other racial minorities to give priority to this problem, but the white leadership of school integration might have recognized it earlier and responded to it.

5. Both legal interpretations and our best guesses about sensible education policy lead us to the reduction of racial isolation as a desirable goal. As we pursue this end we will increasingly come up against very difficult problems of how far to go. Obviously, there are practical limits based upon the distribution of people from different races and backgrounds. The schools do not have full control of the problem because forces outside them dictate where people live and work. Also, there remains the perplexing issue of how to give blacks, Mexican-Americans, Puerto Ricans, and others a sense that the schools belong to them too, that they can lead and operate schools and set their policies as can whites. Those of us who press hardest for desegregation of students tend to lose sight of other matters that also need our attention; the business of getting more minority-group teachers and administrators into the schools also is a priority task.

Let me turn now to what I really want to emphasize in getting at this topic of public education for a humane society, the internal aspects of the school.

Racial and economic integration of educational institutions is a prerequisite for bringing about emphasis on humane values within those institutions. This is so because humane values that include kindness, compassion, and benevolence toward all human beings suffer where there is a policy of exclusion. To the degree that an institution says "no admittance" to some class of persons because of race or color or nationality, it diminishes the chance that those it does admit will have a total sense of humanity. This is the basic argument against segregation, against apartheid. It is based upon the view that physical or cultural differences among men breed fear and suspicion that are passed on from one generation to the next, but that these can be overcome by the rational and civilized attainments of human beings. The schools are especially important because there most of us have our earliest and most impressionable experiences with people outside our own families. Racial prejudice is learned, not inherited, so we need to create an environment for children that will give them the chance to learn mutual respect. It's worth remembering from time to time the irony in the song from the old, but unforgettable, musical show *South Pacific* . . . ["Carefully Taught"].

I labor this point because there has been so much research and argument about whether or not integration produces better reading scores or better mathematics scores or fewer dropouts among minority-group children. Without denying that such studies and debates are worthwhile, I want to assert that there are vastly more significant considerations in the intangible effects on individual children of being segregated or integrated and in addition vastly more significant considerations in the influence of education upon the nature and values of the society. These were the broad grounds upon which the Supreme Court reached its views in the Brown decision of 1954, when in effect it said that separation is incapable of producing equality.

But the battle is far from won when a school enrolls a cross section of Americans among its students. From speeches at this conference, as well as from well-documented experience in countless schools that we describe as "desegregated," we know that *inside* the school young people are experiencing discrimination. In the guidance office, in the testing procedures, in assignment to programs and courses, in the application of discipline, and in countless other ways, there is clear evidence that segregation and discrimination have moved inside the school—probably with greater impact in the secondary schools than the elementary because of the track systems and pupil-assignment practices typical of the upper years of schooling. In recommendations like those of the Fleischman Commission in New York State for the abolition of the so-called "general program," which leads to neither employment nor college and to which so many minority-group young people are relegated, you have evidence of current efforts to attack this interior discrimination, at least in its organizational aspects. The Fleischman Commission's policies should be applauded and supported along with others designed to change the school from an institution that sorts out young people by rejecting some and advancing others to an institution that gives *dignity to all, rejection to none, and a sense of progress to each.*

How then to change schooling more fundamentally than by bringing together children of different races and backgrounds? The first requirement is a transition from *competition* to *cooperation* as the dominant mode and style of the school; and the second is the alteration this shift in values will imply in the authority structure and human relationships within the school.

For many Americans competition is a fundamental principle of life, and there is some tendency among us to equate it with motherhood in the relative scale of values. Our economic system is based on the myth of free competition in the market place, although fortunately for both the businessman and the consumer, they are increasingly protected by government from the excesses that inevitably accompany unbridled competitiveness. Schools are riddled with a faith in the values of competition. This is what undergirds their commitment to interscholastic sports (which deny opportunity to the female 50 percent of the population and to all but a small percentage of males as well) and their use of marking systems (which are frequently arranged to put down as many students as they encourage). It is strongly argued that the best in character and performance is elicited by the competitive instinct. I recall a statement on this matter by that grand old warrior, General Douglas MacArthur:

> It [athletic competition] is a vital character builder. It molds the youth of our country for their future roles as custodians of the republic. It teaches them to be strong enough to know they are weak, and brave enough to face themselves when they are afraid. . . . It gives them a temper of the will, a quality of the imagination, a vigor of the emotions. . . . Fathers and mothers who would make their sons into men should have them play the game.

This sort of windy, sentimental exaggeration is too typical of much of our thinking about competition. The best comment I know on it came from my then seventeen-year-old daughter, who said when I read it to her: "Is he serious?"

If we are to have a humane society anywhere in the world, we shall have to rid ourselves of much of the competitiveness that dominates our every action and decision. On the world scene the dominant, overriding fact is the misery of 75 percent of the world's people as the few luxuriate in affluence. Greater cooperation is the only possible answer to the perils that lie ahead in this explosive contrast. In our own society we are just beginning to face the hard fact that some of us will have to accept less in goods and services if all of us are to have the chance for a reasonable existence. As the energy crisis and environmental problems force themselves upon us in the years ahead, the ethic of competitiveness as productive of the greatest good for the greatest number will come increasingly into question.

So I suggest that the school is one place to start the revolution that is required in our values and behavior in the interest of humane survival. We must seek practical ways in our schools to enhance cooperative endeavors and to reduce destructive competition. If we can give pupils status-producing recognition for what they achieve personally, can't we be clever enough to give equal or greater status for what they contribute to the school, to the class, or to the learning of others? If we extend admiration to teachers for the success of their pupils in academic tasks, can't we include in such recognition some concept of progress so that our praise is extended not just for what the best students achieve, but also in recognition of the more modest attainments of the less able student? His learning problems may have been vastly more difficult for the teacher to diagnose and to overcome, whereas the top achievers might well have succeeded with no assistance from a teacher.

On the too few occasions I have to visit schools, I see some evidence of moves in the directions suggested here. People who work in schools (and particularly in city schools) have been the subject of more criticism and advice from self-appointed experts who never worked in city schools than any other category of professional person I can think of. Now they are beginning to find the ways to help themselves by promoting cooperation among teachers, principals, parents, and pupils, with the purpose of making all children more successful. The endeavors of this nature I have seen have not been organized as massive, system-wide programs. Last month here in New York I visited a place where teachers come together voluntarily to seek ideas and stimulation from each other about how to make their classes more successful. No one was telling them how to do it, but they were encouraged to expand their teaching repertoires. They were devising approaches to learning that would motivate youngsters and enlist them in the learning process. This informal center for helping teachers brings in children, parents, and other community residents. It touches the life of a dozen elementary schools. It proceeds on a non-directive, exploratory, and cooperative basis. It results in classes that emphasize cooperation, as well as giving children much more initiative and responsibility than the usual school. No one knows the effects of all this on reading scores. I suspect that they will improve markedly over time. Meanwhile, the values being demonstrated are important enough to justify the enterprise.

Another school I visited not long ago in a low-income area of Los Angeles had worked out a regular system to have fifth graders working as tutors with second and third graders. The routines and attitudes of teachers, students, administrators, and even parents were all affected by this arrangement. There was clear evidence that reading was improving among both third graders and fifth graders, but more important were the changes that had come about in the human relationships of the school. It was transforming itself into an institution in which people felt responsible for each other and were really engaged on a cooperative basis.

I cite these small examples because for me they carry a clear message about the nature of public education that holds some hope of fostering a humane society. Humaneness is a personal quality. It can't be legislated; it can't be bought; it can't be turned on by massive programs, although leadership that understands it can do much to encourage it. It can be built by people who care and one of the essential building blocks is the gathering together of people from all races and circumstances.

Educational change that will emphasize humane values will have to come from the bottom up. It will have to start with teachers and parents who get together and seek ways both to interest children and to make them more successful. It will involve the pupils themselves in the process. It will depend upon initiatives in the individual school or in small groups of schools in which people know each other well. Massive educational hierarchies at city, state, and national levels will only get in the way unless they learn how to create an atmosphere that supports and frees the initiatives of teachers, parents, administrators, and students in the schools. People within the individual school and school community should have more control than they typically do over the expenditure of the funds that are supposed to be improving education and over the design of programs to make schools more responsive to children. In some cases humane values will enter the schools from sources totally outside them. Spend some time watching "Sesame Street" and "The Electric Company" on TV, if you want to see education for a humane society in action. Happily, these programs reach millions of children.

It is possible, of course, to argue against the replacement of competition by cooperation, to say that this is a competitive world and that the schools will serve children ill unless they prepare them through competition. This argument defends the sorting-out function of the schools, the advancement of some and the rejection of others, partly on grounds that the toughness and resolution needed to contend with the realities of life can be produced only in a competitive environment. The argument contends also that competition is necessary to produce quality in intellectual endeavors. This sort of social Darwinism seems to me utterly fallacious. It assumes that there is no rigor, no discipline, or character development in a cooperative environment. I submit that the opposite is true and that the sense of responsibility, the power of restraint, and the patience an individual must have to function effectively in a cooperative venture are more highly civilized attributes than those produced by competition. Also, they are more useful and more humane. As for the idea that high-quality intellectual endeavor is dependent on competition, on beating the other fellow out for the Nobel prize, or the Phi Beta Kappa key, or the best scholastic average, this is a ridiculously simplistic interpretation of the motivation of scholars.

Before closing these remarks, I want to comment on the relationship between the use and abuse of authority in schools and education for a humane society. Cooperation and the mutual respect and tolerance that are both its product and its source cannot exist in a rigid, authoritarian system. Many pressures today are bending the school toward more rigidities. Occasional or even regular violence calls forth restrictions, policing, and punishments. Threats from the surrounding community force schools to lock their doors against that community, which may be their greatest learning resource. These events breed a vicious circle of threat and heightened response from which there seems no escape. Teachers do need protection and so do students, but the need for basic protection should not be allowed to create a fortress climate in our schools.

There is no easy or quick answer to these conditions and problems. Some of their causes lie deep in the wounds of our society and will continue to operate until those wounds start to heal—among them racial discrimination and segregation. But secure and confident teachers and administrators in schools can begin to find ways to run their institutions in a style that says to students and teachers, "We trust you." Where this message is clear and where the relations among the adults in a school are open, direct, and respectful, there will be a response, and the school will be on the way to useful change and to education for a humane society.

In setting our sights on an integrated society with integrated schools that reflect humane values, we are declaring an idealistic position. That is, we are trying to bring about conditions that a hard-headed view might call difficult, if not impossible, to attain. In doing so we must recognize that idealism is out of fashion these days. It advocates change, raises people's emotional temperatures, and can even be blamed for some of our recent eruptions of social discontent among students and minorities.

So-called practical men are saying: "Forget these visionary goals, be pragmatic, recognize that there's no way to integrate Harlem or to accomplish a hundred other difficult tasks that stand between our present condition and our hopes." They argue that the constant disturbance of the body politic resulting from pressures for racial justice and school reform has become counterproductive on both fronts. "Benign neglect" has even been suggested as the most constructive posture for the national administration in racial affairs.

These warnings and reservations need to be heard by an assembly like the National Conference of Christians and Jews, for they remind each of us of the difficulty and danger of the tasks ahead. In carrying out those tasks there is no place for anger and hate; there is a need for resolution and patience and hard work. But our history provides too many examples of success in producing constructive change in our social institutions to surrender to the doctrine that we should abandon our ideals and accept our imperfections because the task of change is too great. Clearly we have enough difficulties to go around. As the poet A. E. Housman said, "The troubles of our proud and angry dust are from eternity and shall not fail." But the people assembled here, as well as millions of others, have the capacity to bear those troubles and in the process to resolve some of them. That is what it's all about.

THE DECADE OF SHORTCUTS [3]

KINGMAN BREWSTER, JR. [4]

It is probably true that a "new quiet" on college and university campuses has replaced the turbulence and the strife that prevailed during the sixties (see Theodore M. Hesburgh's "Higher Education Begins the Seventies," REPRESENTATIVE AMERICAN SPEECHES: 1970-1971, pages 85-93). Sit-ins and violence became less frequent during 1971-1972. An editorial entitled "Commencement 1972," in the New York *Times,* June 6, 1972, commented:

> An even more fundamental change is the reassessment by students of the academic institutions' lasting values. Much was wrong with higher education when student discontent first exploded at Berkeley back in 1964. Not unlike other national institutions, the universities had grown self-satisfied, set in their ways and often forgetful of their responsibilities toward students and society. But the students have since learned that the universities are not only indispensable but also capable of self-renewal and reform.

Kingman Brewster, Jr., president of Yale University, opened the 1972-1973 school year with a note of optimism when on September 11, 1972, he addressed the Freshman Assembly, an annual event on the Yale campus. He spoke in Woolsey Hall, the main auditorium, to 1,350 incoming freshmen, some 500 parents, the faculty, and guests from the New Haven community. On this occasion, the Yale president, in addition to welcoming the newcomers, offered astute observations on education and problems affecting the nation's colleges. When he finished speaking, the audience gave Brewster strong applause. The speech received good coverage in the newspapers, and the New York *Times* analyzed it editorially and carried a shortened version on its Op-Ed page.

[3] Address delivered at the Freshman Assembly, Yale University, September 11, 1972. Quoted by permission.

[4] For biographical note, see Appendix.

Hopeful that he had read student moods accurately, Brewster sought to inspire the entering freshmen to four years of challenging study:

> In these and in the life of Yale . . . you will make a difference—for good or evil—in the lives of others. . . .
>
> Maybe the highest morality is to achieve some understanding which contributes to the lives of others; or perhaps even to the life of our country or humanity at large.

Brewster sought to direct the students toward the pursuit of liberality and humaneness—forgetting selfish concerns and petty protests. The optimism of the speech is a welcome contrast to the pessimism found in some of the other speeches presented in this volume.

The speech is worthy of careful analysis. First, it is simply organized and well unified, moving toward the speaker's preconceived goal. Second, the language is highly appropriate and vivid. The sentences are carefully fitted together, and some possess an epigrammatic quality. For example, Brewster at one moment says, "And if you are very bright and very lucky and work hard at being both, you may even know the special satisfaction of contributing your light from your own special perspective on some shadowy corner of the universe."

The speech shows why Brewster is considered one of the better academic speakers today.

It is said that there is a "new quiet" settling upon the colleges and universities.

Maybe, but I do not think it runs very deep. Obviously you know better than I what your mood is.

However, I do know something about the moods of your predecessors. There have been three quite different ways in which some students over the last ten years sought to find some exhilaration, some zeal in the undergraduate years. Each patent medicine was somewhat oversold, overindulged in by some; treated with indifference by others. Their prescription has been followed by a measure of disillusionment; yet each overdose has left a residue of change—for the most part constructive change.

One of these nostrums was the cry for "relevance." At best this was an unhappy form of speech, for relevance is a dependent word; it prompts the question: "relevant to what?" The urge was for learning which is concerned with the current ills of the world. Such slogans as "the only purpose of learning is action" left no room for the search for truth or beauty or goodness "for its own sake." The enthusiasm was activist. There was an impatience to work on the immediate and searing problems of peace, poverty, and race, NOW! The cult of relevance was made restless and frustrated by the hard work which it takes to master the disciplines and professions. Yet without such command there is little chance to have much leverage on many social problems. Most particularly the demand for relevance was scornful of history. The paradox was that some of their most far-out faculty mentors were revisionist historians. In many ways the radicalism most relevant to relevance was to be found in the origins of the American republic.

Disillusion with "relevance" set in, I believe, in part because spot news has a high rate of obsolescence. Activist clichés wore pretty thin. Slogans could not long disguise ignorance, and strident impatience was often revealed as a cover for sloppiness. Also, real problems just did not bend to the hot winds of rhetoric; nor did they yield easily to mindless action, no matter how highly motivated.

Nevertheless, the cause of "relevance" did have its positive impact. Some faculty members were persuaded to rethink the significance of what they were doing. The organization of courses and seminars around social problems took its place alongside descriptive and analytical and critical learning based on the single discipline. Perhaps most important, educators were reminded that the motivation for learning can be tremendously heightened if students have more of a chance to design their own programs and are given some chance to fashion experimental seminars which reflected their deepest current concerns.

Carried to its ultimate extreme relevance-worship would destroy liberal education. It would dictate an entirely vocational education. But its championship has required a re-justification of what we do. It has loosened the bonds of what used to be a rigidly prescribed and narrowly departmentalized education.

"Relevance" was a fad; but it left behind a very healthy demand for *significance.* "So what?" is not an inappropriate academic question.

Another campus characteristic running from the mid-sixties into the turn of the decade was the glorification of the "happening." Anything was good as long as it expressed the real, now self. For some, spontaneity was king. For them any critical standards which might give objective definition to the good, the true, or the beautiful were banished. "Doing your thing" was beautiful because it was your very own thing of the moment. "Speaking with tongues" was its apotheosis. This enthusiasm deprecated all manners, modesty, and mentality.

Ultimately, this cult, too, would make the university tradition quite anachronistic. For without reason to monitor the objective search for truth, there is little need or justification for systematic learning or research. You would not need all the paraphernalia of facilities, courses, curricula—let alone grades, credits, and degrees simply to provide a happening.

At the same time the worship of spontaneity did inject a provocative and invigorating influence. It leavened the dry and sometimes arid logic-chopping and footnote-gathering of some rational analysts and the critics. The often defiant irrationality of the "counterculture" has perhaps had the effect of strengthening the defenses of the culture. Also it has awakened all but the most insensitive to a renewed appreciation of those immeasurable dimensions and depths of life which are beyond the power of numbers to describe and of reason to explain. Intuition and imagination, particularly in the arts, have gained a new status in the house of intellect.

In the aftermath of the "living theatre" and the "living classroom," however, there is a yearning for structure; a sense of the emptiness which is left even after a full menu of disorganized experience in the raw.

A third element, which so preoccupied the press and the politicians and the parents (and the college presidents) as the sixties turned into seventies, was the fad of trashing. It brought out the worst in those relatively few who were directly involved. More often than not it set back the cause which was its alleged excuse. It degraded the trashers because it often smacked of exhibitionist tantrum. Its ugliness bred a counterugliness in the backlash of public opinion and the uptightness of official reaction. At best, people looked silly; at worst they were made mean and hateful—on both sides of the barricades.

Fortunately there has been a spreading awareness that violence does not help a cause, and that it more often than not plays into the hands of stubborn, repressive reaction.

Nevertheless much of the demonstrable disobedient protest, especially in its non-violent form, was an important technique of communication when effective expression of concern was felt to be thwarted or stifled by the established channels of politics and authority. When protest was imbued with selflessness and sacrifice rather than egotism and self-congratulation, the message got through when otherwise it might not.

The demand for relevance, the glorification of the happening, the resort to violence all had one thing in common. They were all shortcuts. They were doomed to frustration and letdown, for there are no shortcuts to understanding and understanding is essential to true satisfaction and absolutely crucial to real effectiveness.

Clues to the order and harmony of nature cannot be found without patient mastery of mathematical and experimental disciplines. Even if the ultimate aim is action to preserve the natural condition, to make it more productive or more conducive to a decent human life; the application of science requires first of all command of its mysteries.

The social condition most obviously is riven with problems which defy easy or gimmicky solution. At bottom lies the paradox that there is no freedom without order; yet no order is durable unless its citizens feel that their lot is by and large voluntary. The resolution of this riddle—whether in economic, political, or social terms—cannot be found by idle rumination.

The path to progress cannot detour around the complexities which are at the root of humanity's frustration. There is no easy route to real understanding of the ways in which social, economic and political influence bears down upon the individual through mammoth organizations intricately related by markets and networks of power.

Finally, there is no short cut to an understanding of the personal condition. There is in all of us a crisis of personal purpose. Where are the foundations of enduring satisfaction? Which are the stars we might best steer by? If neither the religious inheritance nor the gospel of wealth or status seem to provide a satisfactory vision of success, there is no simple way to discover our own vision.

There is at least consolation in knowing that we are not alone and need not be embarrassed in our quandary. Where do we look? There is help in the experience and reflections and creations of generation upon generation of each culture's most gifted chroniclers, writers, and artists. Perhaps the clues to purpose are best found in the recorded and expressed experience of others of all places and all ages.

Your years at any university will have their moments of wretchedness and frustration. But these years are a great opportunity to find some new clues to your own most durable purposes and satisfactions.

At least if you apply yourself a bit you should learn the satisfaction of really knowing what you are talking about in some field. And if you are very bright and very lucky and work hard at being both, you may even know the special satisfaction of contributing your own light from your own special perspective on some shadowy corner of the universe. You do not have to be a professional intellectual in order to become genuinely excited by ideas. Even if an idea is not brand new, the excitement of its discovery and the appreciation of its beauty can be your own.

There is more to this place than the life of the mind. Clues to purpose can also be discovered outside the library, the classroom, or the laboratory. The obvious physical overcrowding to which you are all subject was not the conscious design of a perverse paternalism. Quite apart from some of its claustrophobic aspects until the new colleges are built, however, Yale is a community; or more accurately, an array of sub-communities—communities of residence; communities of sport and extracurricular activity; communities of common causes; communities of organized and unorganized societies and associations.

In these and in the life of Yale as a University College, you will make a difference—for good or evil—in the lives of others. Do not let sheepishness or cynicism deny you the moral dimension of this aspect of college life. Admit that you are a moral as well as physical and intellectual being. Make the most of it, enjoy it.

Maybe the highest morality is to achieve some understanding which contributes to the lives of others; or perhaps even to the life of our country or humanity at large.

Almost exactly ten years ago, a Yale graduate who has provoked and stimulated generations of thinkers and learners, Robert Maynard Hutchins, said:

> I believe life without theory has come to an end in the United States. A search for principles has begun. We have been absent-minded. We have to think. And the task of revitalizing the American creed and creatively reinterpreting it and making it once more the light and the hope of the world is primarily an intellectual task.

Maybe we had to go through the decade of shortcuts; relevance, the escape from reason to spontaneity; and for a few, the mad therapy of violence. Certainly they did not reach or even touch the fundamental task. It is still ahead of us. We need a theory which makes sense of our universe, our society, and ourselves. Whatever part of that search is yours, by dint of preparation, competence or interest, do not forget the magnificence of the challenge.

OPPORTUNITY FOR EDUCATIONAL INNOVATION [5]

MATINA S. HORNER [6]

Matina S. Horner was installed as the sixth president of Radcliffe College, November 16, 1972. On that occasion she gave her inaugural address at Agassiz House on the Radcliffe College campus, Cambridge, Massachusetts.

As the incoming president of a distinguished women's college, Dr. Horner faced a friendly audience but a difficult educational problem. At the present time, when emphasis is being placed upon equality of the sexes and upon integration, there has been much talk about the phasing out of special colleges and universities for women and blacks. Already many such institutions have disappeared or have been restructured. Changing admissions policies often mean that women's colleges soon become coeducational. The speaker recognized these pressures when she observed that "our two institutions [Radcliffe and Harvard] resisted the temptation to follow national trends . . . for complete coeducation—total merger." Lynn Sakai, president of the class of 1973, was aware of this problem when she greeted the new president: "We [the class of 1973] have been politicized from all sides—the Quadrangle, the Yard, the River. We do not have a shared past, but we have experiences to share. We must carefully encourage the new merging Radcliffe identity. Let us create a Radcliffe community here at Harvard."

Not only sensitive to these trends but also aware that specialized education for women has been challenged, Dr. Horner discussed the role that Radcliffe would play in "the new society." The review of the institution's ninety-year history gave support to her thesis that the college has a continuing role to play.

The organization of the speech was excellent. In the third paragraph the speaker set forth a preview of how she intended to develop her thought: "to reflect upon the tradition of the past, to recognize and respond to the needs of the present and to consider . . . the future." In the remainder of the speech she proceeded to follow this organization.

[5] Address delivered November 16, 1972, at Radcliffe College, Cambridge, Massachusetts. Quoted by permission.

[6] For biographical note, see Appendix.

On this formal occasion the speaker made her presentation more attractive by inserting specific references to her family and particularly to her six-year-old son. Hence she enhanced her persuasiveness. The speech was an excellent academic address. The *Harvard University Gazette* (November 17, 1972) reported that the speaker "read" her speech "quickly," and that she "held the attention even of her youngest son, Chris."

The audience included His Eminence Archbishop Iakovos of the Greek Orthodox Church. He had known the Radcliffe president since she was a child.

I come before you today with high expectations and, to a certain extent, some anxiety. You have entrusted Radcliffe's future to me, and I hope that I shall prove worthy of your confidence and trust.

Together we celebrate this moment in Radcliffe's history as a family. My only sense of regret is that *all* our students could not be here with us. It is for us all an opportunity for serious contemplation about and thanksgiving for the nature and quality of our "Acre for Education."

It is an opportunity to pause from the busy-ness of the day's activities, to reflect upon the traditions of the past, to recognize and respond to the needs of the present, and to consider the possibilities of the future.

These are exciting and challenging times for those of us concerned with higher education in general and with the education of women in particular. We are aware that today many social, sexual, and vocational changes are occurring in society with such awesome acceleration that many more questions are raised than we can immediately answer. Among other questions under consideration, one of particular importance to Radcliffe is what role women will play in the new society. Her relation to work, study and family is under close scrutiny and review, and reactions of both sexes toward her new social importance are varied. In the light of Radcliffe's long tradition of improving opportunities for women who have "the taste and talent for higher education," we at the College must now enter a new and intensely self-critical period, directing our attention toward re-evaluating our goals and defining our objectives. If we do so, mindful of the issues of our times, we can shape and provide an environment here that will help prepare young women and men to meet the demanding academic and social pressures which change has brought. It will not be easy. The new demands on the educator to assist students to surmount the many educational and psychological Mount Everests they now face in college and beyond will require new and unpracticed skills. Our aim is to create a living and learning environment in which each student can experience the joy of discovering her own capabilities. Our hope is to create a community in and out of which each student—past, present and future—can realize the fulfillment of her talent and the fullness of her spirit. I will be happy when we have reached the point in society that a woman is appointed or gains admission to respected, high-level positions not in spite of, nor because of the fact that she is a woman but because she is, feels, and is recognized to be a talented human being with something important to give.

Your Eminence, I am delighted that you could be here today—not only because of the fond memories your presence evokes for me personally, but also because it serves as a reminder to us all of how far we have come. The clergy, as you know, has not always looked kindly on women educators and speakers. In 1837, the General Association of Congregational Churches in Massachusetts issued a Pastoral Letter in which they declared quite firmly:

> We cannot . . . but regret the mistaken conduct of those who encourage females to bear an obtrusive and ostentatious role and who countenance any of that sex to so far forget themselves as to itinerate in the character of public lecturers and teachers.

I shudder to think of their reactions to the events of this day.

Despite the presence of such attitudes, not only in the clergy but even among members of the Harvard faculty and Governing Boards, Radcliffe's early leaders remained undaunted. Committed to the idea that women could, and therefore should, be educated like men, Mr. Gilman and Mrs. Agassiz organized a plan for providing "private, collegiate instruction for women . . ." equal to the best available for men: namely, that at Harvard. They sought instruction that was not only to be of Harvard quality, but to be given by Harvard teachers and lead to certification recognized as equal to a Harvard degree. Because they challenged the existing stereotypes and expectations of their time, they met considerable resistance. The resistance was based on arguments such as the one that female education could only be gained at the expense of woman's reproductive function, and that academic and public achievement could only be realized at the expense of a woman's femininity, marriage and family. These are not unlike the arguments one hears today.

Dr. Edward Clarke, for instance, a Professor of Medicine at Harvard and later an Overseer of the College, argued at that time that while a boy could study for six hours a day, if a girl spent more than four, her "brain or special apparatus" would suffer.

Similarly, President Eliot remained firm in his conviction that the physique of woman was unfit for higher education despite the statement from Vassar in 1873 that "four hundred healthier women can hardly be found than those at Poughkeepsie."

And yet, our predecessors persisted and ultimately established a college for women in Harvard's backyard, in a location described as "up the river from Boston and down through the forest from Watertown." The founders won President Eliot's support for their plan when they assured him that they all opposed coeducation and that the plan would in no way strain Harvard's finances. It would, they argued, enhance the College's attraction for outstanding faculty members by providing an additional source of income. I am amused, in the context of today's fiscal crisis, to learn that at one time Radcliffe was considered a "financial temptress." But, I am digressing. . . .

Arguments that Radcliffe was founded in quicksand and doomed to end in failure or complete coeducation proved to be unfounded. Instead, "gradually, steadily, miraculously, with no convulsion of nature, the quicksand hardened into rock," proving that women could be educated with, and on the same campus as, men without suffering the severe physical or mental aberrations predicted, and even without introducing an "element of frivolity into the serious business of education."

Times and attitudes have changed. President Bok's remarks to the Class of '76 attest to that fact. Commenting on this year's historic event—the official introduction of two hundred freshwomen into the Harvard Yard—he said:

> I am confident that the civilizing influence of these two hundred pioneers will produce an aura of graciousness and scholarly dedication never before achieved upon that hallowed ground.

For ninety years, Radcliffe's historic and continuing contribution has been to make accessible to women the opportunities afforded by a Harvard education—an education anchored in more than three centuries of excellence. Our connection with Harvard was then and continues to be essential to our progress. I, for one, am glad that she is there and that she has the kind of leadership she does in men like Derek Bok and John Dunlop.

With courage and foresight, my predecessors met the challenging problems of educating women in their time and succeeded in opening the doors of quality education to them. This goal is no longer sufficient. The challenge to our generation is different and, in some ways, considerably more complex. Many of the issues at stake involve intangibles. We have, for instance, a culture and an educational system that ostensibly encourage and prepare men and women identically for educational programs and careers which, evidence indicates, other social and psychological pressures really limit to men.

We pride ourselves on being completely free of the prejudices of the age in which Radcliffe was founded, and yet experience and recent research, including my own, tell us differently.

I remind you that it was *1968* when Anthony Storr stated in his highly acclaimed and respected book, *Human Aggression,* that:

> . . . it is highly probable that the undoubted superiority of the male sex in intellectual and creative achievement is related to their greater endowment of aggression. . . . The hypothesis that women, if only given the opportunity and encouragement, would equal or surpass the creative achievements of men is hardly defensible.

And it was *1970* when Dr. Edgar Berman said of women:

> Their physical and psychological disabilities render them unfit to make important decisions or hold positions of power.

With the existence of such attitudes, it is not surprising to find that young men and women of today still tend to evaluate themselves and behave in ways consistent with age-old stereotypes and expectations. These stereotypes argue that independence, competence, intellectual achievement and leadership are all positive attributes of maturity and mental health. These very characteristics are at the same time viewed as synonymous with what is male and as basically inconsistent with what is female. The implication is that a feminine woman cannot be a healthy, mature adult and Margaret Mead's statement that "each step forward as a successful American is a step back as a woman" is very much to the point.

Thus, one of the challenges to our generation will be to help women resist and dissolve the persistent myth that the development of their intellectual capacity and the fulfillment of any of their nontraditional aspirations is a denial of their femininity and proof of their inadequacy as potential wives and mothers. This myth prevents educated women from walking through doors now open to them, from exercising their skills in personally meaningful and satisfying ways, and from taking advantage of opportunities now available to them. What a tremendous waste of both human and economic resources this represents! The price is too high. It is paid for by our students and by women in general in an easily recognizable loss of confidence and self-esteem, in an attrition of aspirations, in a persistence of low expectations for the future, and in the presence of a pervasive, often self-defeating sense that they are second-class citizens. These are impossible conditions for personal and intellectual growth and development.

It has become increasingly clear that only if all our students (both men and women) leave here feeling confident about their own abilities and about their capacity to *freely* determine the directions of their future lives, will they be stimulated toward creative involvement with the world about them. Only then will society be able to meet the steadily increasing demand for the talent necessary to identify and solve some of the major problems of the day—problems like pollution, overpopulation, health and child care delivery, and changing styles of life and learning in the community.

Obviously we cannot undo the impact of child-rearing practices that families have followed and that our institutions have reinforced for years. I do believe, however, that it will be possible, though not easy, with imaginative educational programs to help our students develop a strong sense of their worth, gain confidence in themselves as they master academic and social skills, and ultimately counteract the tendency to withdraw from the mainstream of thought and achievement in our society. In essence, this is the task I see before me.

Since I have assumed this office, one of the questions I have been asked most frequently is: What do I do and how do I spend my day?

From the perspective of my six-year-old, I was intrigued to learn last week that I spend my time writing "dumb speeches," and when not so creatively occupied, am in my office "making ideas." I then remember hoping that his perception of today's effort was not prophetic and that the opportunity for "making ideas" could be more frequent.

Another perspective on the job of a modern college president comes from Henry Wriston of Brown University. He said in 1946 that

> the president is expected to be an educator, to have been at some time a scholar, to have judgment about finances, to know something of construction, maintenance, and labor policy, to speak virtually continuously in words that charm and never offend, to take bold positions with which no one will disagree, to consult with everyone and follow all proferred advice, and do everything through committees, but with great speed and without error.

I must say that there are times when I am certain Mr. Wriston anticipated the true dimensions of my job, *except* for the additional expectations that arise if the president is a woman. To paraphrase Marya Mannes, no one will object to a woman being president *if,* in addition to her official duties, she manages to "be a good wife, a good mother, good looking, good tempered, well dressed, well groomed, and unaggressive."

In the wake of such fulsome observations and expectations, you may wonder, as so many have, why *on* earth I took on this job. I must admit that I was tempted not *in spite of* but *because of* the unique nature of our present relationship with Harvard.

Our two institutions resisted the temptation to follow national trends or to succumb to pressures—political, financial and federal—for complete coeducation—total merger. They have thus given us an especially great opportunity for educational innovation. I, for one, am grateful for and excited by it. Ours together is an unique "experiment in education," as Mrs. Agassiz called it—*unique* in the possibility it provides (if only we take advantage of it) for identifying and bringing together the best aspects of independent single-sex and coeducational institutions—and of developing here the kind of living and learning environment that sufficient time, effort and adequate information will tell us are not only helpful but essential in preparing our extraordinarily talented students for their roles in the rapidly changing world about them.

There are at the moment many more questions than there are answers. But only if we consciously and actively take the time and effort—*now*—to raise the questions, to pursue the answers and to evaluate their implications will we be able to have a valuable and valid input in the lives of our students and through them to the wider society and toward the solution of its many problems.

I feel a particular responsibility to respond to this exciting challenge and to bring to fruition what three invigorating years of research, teaching and learning in this faculty have taught me. Observing the exciting young men and women in our student body engaged in vital dialogue with the intriguing questions of life and learning, I have become convinced that the full development and achievement of our students depends not only on the quality of the *academic* programs we offer them but also, and perhaps even more importantly, on the subtle attitudes and expectations held by those around them—by the faculty that teach them, by the advisors that counsel them and by the administrators that admit them. The time has come to ask the vexing questions —whether, when, or how one teaches men and women differently, *not* in standards of accomplishment *nor* in content, but in pedagogical technique. We must do so, so that the energy and talents of the students are not exhausted in a struggle against either overt and covert discrimination in such areas as admissions, curricular or extra-curricular opportunity, and that they are not frustrated because certain activities and behavior carry masculine or feminine label, either explicitly or implicitly.

In the end, the success of our "educational experiment" and the quality of the programs we create will be judged by their ability to give all students, male and female alike, the freedom to develop and employ their talents and energies in harmony with self-determined life goals. Our students can give their best to society only if they are able to pursue programs, careers and ways of life they find personally rewarding and socially worthwhile—and to do so in an atmosphere free of the pressure to conform to existing stereotypes—*past* and *present.*

The days have gone when Sophocles could have his player say: "Woman, a woman's ornament is silence." The world that permitted a woman to live, in Robert Frost's words, "Hopeless of being known for what she has been, failing of being loved for what she is" has perished, or soon will. In its place, Radcliffe, and other institutions like it, must mold and shape and found a world where the opportunities open to men and women, the hopes they can share and the new society they can create together will flourish. What we do here will be seen and studied by many. As we join together today as a family, we find ourselves with an important challenge, the challenge of shaping the intellectual and personal development of the young men and women who will ultimately determine the new directions of this society.

You have made me responsible for answering this challenge, and I look forward to your help in this effort.

In conclusion, as I formally accept my new responsibilities, I must say a word of thanks and praise to the members of my family—to my parents and especially to my husband Joe and my children, Tia, John and Chris. It is only with their constant reassurance that I have been able to enjoy the task of the presidency, and only with their unending support and patience that I can carry its burdens.

I thank you all for the support, help and confidence with which you have welcomed me both for Radcliffe and for women everywhere. I gladly await the opportunity to work with you in the years ahead and hope that in the not too distant future we shall be able to come together once again as a family and rejoice in what we have accomplished.

FINDING AMERICA [7]

GEORGE B. HARTZOG, JR. [8]

Commencement talks are generally difficult to prepare and even more difficult to deliver. The graduates for whom the ceremony is supposedly planned are usually more eager to get their diplomas than they are to listen to a speech—no matter how famous or eloquent the speaker. The length of the proceedings—with the awarding of degrees—sometimes contributes to restlessness and weariness.

Invited to lend distinction to the day, the speaker must be adroit in finding ways to stir inspiration without seeming trite, without widening the generation gap, and without boring the faculty. In the university of today with its large graduating classes, the speaker perhaps should not hope to touch his throng of listeners very deeply.

George B. Hartzog, Jr., director of the National Park Service, faced these and other problems when he spoke May 27, 1972, at the spring commencement of the University of Arizona. He spoke to an audience of approximately ten thousand, of whom about half were receiving degrees. His listeners occupied the forty-thousand-seat U-shaped Arizona stadium, which was decorated at ground level with a backdrop of plants and with flying pennants representing the fourteen colleges of the university. The magnitude of the setting and the distance between speaker and listeners must have made Hartzog feel remote and greatly aware of the challenge.

In his development the speaker sought to stir understanding between the generations, expressing the essence of his thought in the following paragraph:

> We must preserve the independence of the youthful spirit and the continuing values of the past. For every future is shaped by the past. Only in knowing the past may we judge wisely what is obsolete and what is not, what to discard and what to preserve.

[7] Address delivered at the spring commencement, University of Arizona, Tucson. Quoted by permission.

[8] For biographical note, see Appendix.

This speech showed how a speaker may use amplification to enlarge and to magnify his central theme. The Greek rhetorician Longinus spoke of amplification as the device that "gives a powerful conception of the subject under discussion by causing the mind to dwell upon it." What Hartzog did was to cast his theme in different forms; each presented the listener another view to consider. In fact, in the quoted paragraph he states the same thought in three different ways—each, of course, in different language. Throughout the speech he inserted well-selected quotations to add dimension to his theme. He hoped to strike a balance between reaching the students and giving the older listeners a feeling of worth and importance. But he wisely permitted those present to draw upon their own imaginations for their own private meanings and feelings. A part of the speaker's skill was demonstrated in the shortness of the speech.

A well-known journalist recently returned from a journey across the country and published an account of his search for America. His report seemed to give evidence that he was not entirely sure that he had really found America. But he is not the only one having difficulty in finding America today.

Down through our history Americans have consistently sought to "find" themselves—from Huckleberry Finn to the Easy Rider. And finding one's own identity may not be far different from finding America.

Each generation looks at the world through the prism of its own experiences, and the present always is in some conflict with the past. My own generation came to maturity at a time of great trouble. Our economic system had collapsed; totalitarian dictatorship ruled vast lands and ancient peoples; ruthless aggression destroyed hope for peace; and, we went to war.

Today, a new generation has grown up in a world of similar anxieties and profound social discontent.

Vocal members of this generation have framed a troubled indictment, that the American social and political system has lost its relevance in the face of rapid and pervasive changes.

They say there are two Americas in our midst: the one, affluent and indifferent—able to spend billions of dollars in order that men might walk on the moon and wage tragic war here on earth; the other, marked by inequality of opportunity, hunger, unemployment and educational deprivations particularly, among the submerged one fourth of our population.

They seek to humanize our institutions, to broaden the base of participation and to open to all the avenues of opportunity. Filled with impatience and indignation over the failure of America to be what it is capable of being, their harsh rhetoric is often characterized as the Generation Gap.

Generations, I suggest, have rarely understood each other. Why else should Moses have said: "Honor thy father and mother"? I am sure that was *not* because fathers and mothers were being honored consistently in Biblical times!

Gibran's widely read book *The Prophet* treats of the so-called "generation gap" by suggesting:

> Your children are not your children. They are the sons and daughters of life's longing for itself.
>
> They come through you but not from you. And though they are with you they belong not to you.
>
> You may give them your love but not your thoughts, for they have their own thoughts.
>
> You may house their bodies but not their souls, for their souls dwell in the house of tomorrow which you cannot visit.

Surely Gibran is correct in suggesting that each of us is unique. Each must build his own house—and live in it!

History mocks those who suggest, however, that the past is wholly dreadful and ignoble.

It is from beachheads secured at great personal sacrifice by individuals and generations gone before that society has been able to find the higher ground. Each of our lives has been enriched by the works of a Gandhi, a Rembrandt and a Woody Guthrie.

We must preserve the independence of the youthful spirit and the continuing values of the past. For every future is shaped by the past. Only in knowing the past may we judge wisely what is obsolete and what is not, what to discard and what to preserve.

In planning for a celebration of the Bicentennial of our Republic, all are agreed on one thing—the American Revolution is not yet over! Americans have always had a dream of the better life. Both the young and the old share the burden of transferring that dream and the vitality of civilization from one generation to another.

As Aristotle observed: "Youth has a long time before it and a short past behind: on the first day of one's life one has nothing at all to remember and can only look forward." By contrast, the elderly "live by memory rather than hope; for what is left to them of life is little compared with the long past."

The capacity to love and to cherish ideals with intransigent commitment is a marvelous trait of youth. On the other hand, the wisdom and earthbound experience that come with age, are necessary balance wheels on the soaring fantasy, the untested ideas and the despair of youth.

Surely, we are in the midst of a revolutionary period that is literally a watershed of history. Isolated from our natural and cultural inheritance by a brutal network of concrete and asphalt, dehumanized by a heartless technology that has robbed us of personal identification, we are asking anew the questions: "Who am I?" "Where have I come from?" "Where am I going?" "What am I contributing?" and "Where shall I find America?"

One of our great novelists, a genius constantly in search of America, Thomas Wolfe, spoke for all generations when he said:

> Out of the billion forms of America, out of the savage violence and the dense complexity of all its swarming life; from the unique and single substance of this land and this life of ours, must we draw the power and energy of our own life, the articulation of our speech, the substance of our art.

Ours is a society in which scientific knowledge is a chief source of wealth and power. But what the environmental crisis tells us is that this Nation's future, as President Nixon has emphasized, rests upon new and profoundly fundamental judgments of how this knowledge, and the power that it creates, shall be used.

In our searching inquiry into the causes of a deteriorating environment, we must seek to articulate an environmental ethic to guide personal and corporate conduct.

We must come to believe that the just use of science is not to conquer nature, but to live in harmony with it. We may yet learn that to save ourselves we must save the world, which is our habitat.

Recently, William Pennel Rock, a descendant of Francis Scott Key, who had determined to be an alien for the rest of his life, returned to America after a voluntary exile of seven years. He observed:

> What is utterly unique about America is that dissent—the challenge to moral values, the modification of alternatives, the criticism of cultural standards—is taking place within the context of the American situation as a whole.
>
> It is a fact that only America has the basic elasticity to change its cultural structure at this incredible pace because the margin of revolutionary action, cultural, social and institutional—that is freedom—is greater in America than in any other country.
>
> America . . . is proving its greatness by exercising the capacity to call itself into question.

As you set out to revise and rebuild the Establishment into which you are about to enter, I suggest that you do not deny your birthright, nor reject the proud heritage which is rightfully yours.

This land of ours is a noble land. It is rich not only in its natural inheritance, but in the stories and legends which are its history. Here and there, scattered across the country, are the milestones left behind by men and women seeking to "Find America."

These pioneer Americans hammered out a way of life which continues to provide hope to a troubled world.

Henceforth, from this joyous occasion you join the continuing search to "Find America."

Today is your opportunity for greatness!

Go, then. Build your houses of tomorrow.

In them may you experience a new quality in life.

May you, through your example, establish a new ethic, by which we may live in harmony with our world and with each other.

APPENDIX

BIOGRAPHICAL NOTES

BREWSTER, KINGMAN, JR. (1919-). Born, Longmeadow, Massachusetts; A.B., Yale University, 1941; LL.B., magna cum laude, Harvard University, 1948; LL.D., American International College, 1961; lieutenant, USNR (aviation), 1942-46; assistant to Professor Milton Katz, with Marshall Plan in Europe, 1948-49; research associate, department of economics and social science, Massachusetts Institute of Technology, 1949-50; assistant professor, Harvard Law School, 1950-53; professor, 1953-61; provost, Yale University, 1961-63; president, 1963- ; member, President's Materials Policy Commission, 1951; President's Commission on Law Enforcement and Administration of Justice, 1965; National Advisory Commission on Selective Service, 1966; member, Massachusetts Bar Association, American Academy of Arts and Sciences, Council on Foreign Relations; director, American Council of Learned Societies; author, *Antitrust and American Business Abroad,* 1959; *The Law of International Transactions and Relations* (with Milton Katz), 1960. (See also: *Current Biography: May 1964.*)

CHISHOLM, SHIRLEY (1924-). Born, Brooklyn, New York; B.A., cum laude, Brooklyn College, 1946; M.A., Columbia University, 1952; Professional Diploma in Supervision and Administration, Columbia University, 1960; member, debating society, Brooklyn College; nursery school teacher and director, 1946-53; director, Hamilton-Madison Child Care Center, New York, 1953-59; educational consultant, Division of Day Care, Bureau of Child Welfare, New York City, 1959-64; member, New York State Assembly, 1965-68; US House of Representatives (Democrat, New York), 1969- ; sought Democratic nomination for Presidency, 1972. (See also *Current Biography: October 1969.*)

CLIFFORD, CLARK M. (1906-). Born, Fort Scott, Kansas; LL.B., Washington University, St. Louis, 1928; admitted to the Missouri bar and the District of Columbia bar; private law practice in St. Louis, 1928-50; USNR, 1944-46; naval aide to President, 1946; special counsel to President, 1946-50; senior partner, Clifford and Miller, Washington, D.C., 1950-68; US Secretary of Defense, 1968-69; senior partner, Clifford, Warnke, Glass, McIlwain and Finney, Washington, D.C., 1969- ; recipient, Medal of Freedom. (See also *Current Biography: September 1968.*)

DUBOS, RENÉ J. (1901-). Born, Saint-Brice-sous-Forêt, France; student, College Chaptal, Paris, 1915-19; Institut National Agronomique, Paris, 1919-21; served in French army, 1921-22; assistant, editorial staff, International Institute of Agriculture, Rome, 1922-24; came to United States, 1924; naturalized, 1938; research assistant, soil microbiology, New Jersey Experimental Station, Rutgers University, 1924-27; Ph.D., Rutgers University, 1927; fellow, Rockefeller Institute of Medical Research, 1927-28; assistant, 1928-30; associate, 1930-38; associate member, 1938-41; member, 1941-42, 1944-56; George Fabyan Professor of Comparative Pathology and Professor of Tropical Medicine, Harvard Medical School, 1942-44; member and professor, Rockefeller University for Medical Research, 1957-71; recipient of twenty-six honorary degrees and numerous awards; author, *The Bacterial Cell,* 1945; *Man Adapting,* 1965; *So Human an Animal* (Pulitzer Prize), 1968; *A God Within,* 1972; and other works. (See also *Current Biography: October 1952.*)

GARDNER, JOHN W. (1912-) Born, Los Angeles, California; A.B., Stanford University, 1935; A.M., 1936; Ph.D., University of California, 1938; many honorary degrees; teaching assistant in psychology, University of California, 1936-38; instructor, Connecticut College, 1938-40; assistant professor, Mt. Holyoke College, 1940-42; head, Latin-American section, FCC, 1942-43; USMCR, 1943-46; staff member, Carnegie Corporation, New York, 1946-47; executive associate, 1947-49; vice president, 1949-55; president, 1955-65; consultant, 1968-70; president, Carnegie Foundation for the Advancement of Teaching, 1955-65; US Secretary of Health, Education, and Welfare, 1965-68; chairman, Urban Coalition, 1968-70; chairman, Common Cause, 1970- ; member, Woodrow Wilson Foundation, 1960-63; recipient, USAF Exceptional Services Award, 1956; Presidential Medal of Freedom, 1964; author, *Excellence: Can We Be Equal and Excellent Too?,* 1961; *Self-Renewal: The Individual and the Innovative Society,* 1964; *No Easy Victories,* 1968; *Recovery of Confidence,* 1970; editor, *To Turn the Tide,* 1962. (See also *Current Biography: March 1956.*)

HARTZOG, GEORGE B., JR. (1920-). Born, Colleton County, South Carolina; B.S., American University, 1953; LL.D. (honorary), Washington University, St. Louis, 1971; admitted to practice before the Supreme Court of South Carolina, 1942; US Supreme Court, 1949; Missouri Supreme Court, 1963; with Bureau of Land Management and National Park Service, US Department of the Interior, 1946-62; executive director, Downtown St. Louis, Inc., 1962-63; associate director, National Park Service, 1963-64; director, 1964- ; trustee, John F. Kennedy Center for the Performing Arts, 1964- ;

serves on historical preservation committees in Washington, D.C. (See also *Current Biography: July 1970.)*

HATFIELD, MARK O. (1922-). Born, Dallas, Oregon; A.B., Willamette University, 1943; LL.D., 1958; A.M., Stanford University, 1948; numerous honorary degrees; USNR, 1943-46; resident assistant, Stanford University, 1947-49; instructor, Willamette University, 1949; dean of students, associate professor of political science, 1950-56; member, Oregon House of Representatives, 1951-55; Oregon Senate, 1955-57; secretary of state, Oregon, 1957-59; governor, 1959-67; member, US Senate (Republican, Oregon), 1967- . (See also *Current Biography: November 1959.)*

HORNER, MATINA SOURETIS (1939-). Born, New York City; B.A., cum laude, Bryn Mawr College, 1961; M.S., University of Michigan, 1963; Ph.D., 1968; teaching fellow, University of Michigan, 1962-66; lecturer, 1968; lecturer, Department of Social Relations, Harvard University, 1969; assistant professor of clinical psychology, 1970; consultant to the University Health Services, 1971; associate professor of psychology and social relations, 1972; president of Radcliffe College, 1972- ; elected as an Outstanding Educator of America, 1972. (See also *Current Biography: July 1973.*)

HOWE, HAROLD, II (1918-). Born, Hartford, Connecticut; A.B., Yale University, 1940; M.A., Columbia University, 1947; additional work, University of Cincinnati, 1953-57; Harvard University, 1960; LL.D., Princeton University, 1968; USNR, 1941-45; teacher, Darrow School, New Lebanon, New York, 1940-41; Phillips Academy, Andover, Massachusetts, 1947-50; principal, Andover junior high school, 1950-53; Walnut Hills high school, Cincinnati, 1953-57; Newton (Massachusetts) high school, 1957-60; superintendent of schools, Scarsdale, New York, 1960-64; director, North Carolina Learning Institute, 1964-65; US Commissioner of Education, 1965-68; vice president, Division of Education and Research, Ford Foundation, 1969- ; trustee, College Entrance Examination Board; Yale University; member, Commission on the Humanities. (See also *Current Biography: November 1967.)*

JOHNSON, LYNDON BAINES (1908-1973). Born near Stonewall, Texas; graduate, Johnson City (Texas) high school, 1924; B.S., Southwest Texas State Teachers College, San Marcos, 1930; teacher, public schools, Houston, 1930-31; secretary to Representative Richard M. Kleberg, 1931-35; student, Georgetown Law School,

1935-36; state director, National Youth Administration of Texas, 1935-37; member, US House of Representatives (Democrat, Texas), 1937-48; US Senate, 1949-61; minority leader, eighty-third Congress; majority leader, eighty-fourth—eighty-sixth Congresses; resigned from Senate, January 3, 1961; Vice President of the United States, 1961-63; became President of the United States upon the assassination of President John F. Kennedy, November 22, 1963; President, 1965-69; died January 22, 1973. (See also *Current Biography: March 1964.*)

JORDAN, VERNON E., JR. (1935-). Born, Atlanta, Georgia; B.A., DePauw University, 1957; first prize, Indiana Interstate Oratorical Contest, sophomore year; LL.D., Howard University, 1960; circuit vice president of American Law Students Association while at Howard University; helped to desegregate the University of Georgia; clerk in law office of civil rights attorney Donald Hollowell; field secretary, NAACP, Georgia branch, 1962; set up law partnership in Arkansas with another civil rights lawyer, Wiley A. Barnton, 1964; director, Voter Education Project for the Southern Regional Council, 1964-68; executive director, United Negro College Fund, 1970-72; director, National Urban League, January 1972- ; member, Arkansas and Georgia bar associations; US Supreme Court bar; American Bar Association; Common Cause; Rockefeller Foundation; Twentieth Century Fund; other service organizations; has held fellowships at Harvard University's Institute of Politics, the John F. Kennedy School of Government, and the Metropolitan Applied Research Center. (See also *Current Biography: February 1972.*)

MATHIAS, CHARLES MCCURDY, JR. (1922-). Born, Frederick, Maryland; graduated, Frederick high school, 1939; US Navy, 1942-46; B.A., Haverford College, 1944; LL.B., University of Maryland, 1949; partner, Mathias, Mathias & Michel, Frederick, 1949-53; assistant attorney general of Maryland, 1953-54; member, US Supreme Court bar, 1954; city attorney, Frederick, 1954-59; member, House of Delegates, Maryland, 1958; partner, Niles, Barton, Markell and Gans, Baltimore, 1960- ; member, US House of Representatives (Republican, Maryland), 1961-67; US Senate, 1968- . (See also *Current Biography: December 1972.*)

MCGOVERN, GEORGE S. (1922-). Born, Avon, South Dakota; B.A., Dakota Wesleyan University, 1945; pilot, USAAF; recipient, Distinguished Flying Cross; M.A., Northwestern University, 1949; Ph.D., 1953; professor of history and political science, Dakota

Wesleyan University, 1949-53; executive secretary, Democratic party, South Dakota, 1953-65; member, US House of Representatives (Democrat, South Dakota), 1957-61; special assistant to the President and director, Food for Peace Program, 1961-62; member, US Senate, 1963- ; Democratic candidate for President, 1972; author, *The Colorado Coal Strike, 1913-14*, 1953; *War Against Want*, 1964; *A Time of War, A Time of Peace*, 1968; and other works. (See also *Current Biography: March 1967*.)

PEDEN, WILLIAM (1913-). Born, New York City; B.S., University of Virginia, 1934; M.S., 1936; Ph.D., 1942; instructor, University of Maryland, 1938-42; assistant professor, 1942-44; associate professor, University of Missouri, 1946-50; professor, 1950- ; visiting professor, University of New Mexico, 1955-56; University of Maryland, 1971; director, Writing Program, University of Missouri, 1946- ; director, University of Missouri Press, 1958-62; editorial board, 1962- ; Guggenheim Fellowship, 1962-63; Fulbright Fellowship, 1964; McConnell Foundation Thomas Jefferson Award, 1972; has served on boards of several national writing contests; author, *Short Fiction: Shape and Substance*, 1971; *Twilight at Monticello*, 1973; and other works; editor, *Notes on the State of Virginia*, 1954, and other works.

POWELL, LEWIS FRANKLIN, JR. (1907-). Born, Suffolk, Virginia; B.S., Washington and Lee University, 1929; LL.B., 1931; LL.D., 1960; LL.M., Harvard University, 1932; member, Virginia bar, 1931; US Supreme Court bar, 1937; partner, Hunton, Williams, Gay, Powell and Gibson, 1937-71; justice, US Supreme Court, 1971- ; chairman, special Charter Commission for City of Richmond, charter approved 1947; trustee, member of executive committee, general counsel for Colonial Williamsburg, Inc.; served USAAF, 1942-46; recipient, Legion of Merit; Bronze Star; member, Phi Beta Kappa; Omicron Delta Kappa. (See also *Current Biography: February 1965*.)

REID, LOREN (1905-). Born, Gilman City, Missouri; A.B., Grinnell College, 1927; A.M., 1930; Ph.D., University of Iowa, 1932; high school teacher; assistant professor, University of Missouri, 1935-37; associate professor, Syracuse University, 1939-44; professor, University of Missouri, 1944- ; chairman, speech department, 1947-52, 1966-67; visiting professor (Hawaii, Maryland, Southern California, Utah, Michigan, San Diego State, Iowa); executive secretary, Speech Association of America, 1945-51; president, 1957; recipient, Grinnell College Alumni award, 1962; author of numerous books and articles including, *Charles James Fox*, 1969

(James A. Winans Award); *Studies in American Public Address,* 1961; *Teaching Speech* (fourth edition, 1971).

RUCKELSHAUS, JILL E. (STRICKLAND) (1937-). Born, Indianapolis, Indiana; A.B. with honors, Indiana University, 1958; M.A., Harvard University, 1959; attended law school, Indiana University, 1963-66; teacher, Gstaad, Switzerland, 1959-61; Indiana Central College, 1961-62; teacher and director, Sheltered Workshop, Noble School for Retarded, Indianapolis, 1962-63; special assistant to Anne Armstrong (counselor to President Nixon), 1973- .

RUSK, DEAN (1909-). Born, Cherokee County, Georgia; A.B., magna cum laude, Davidson College, 1931; B.S., St. John's College, Oxford University (Rhodes scholar), 1933; M.A., 1934; LL.D., Mills College, 1948; other honorary degrees; associate professor of government, and dean, Mills College, 1934-40; assistant chief, Division of International Security Affairs, US Department of State, 1946; special assistant to Secretary of War, 1946-47; director, Office of United Nations Political Affairs, US Department of State, 1947-49; Assistant Secretary of State, February 1949; Deputy Under Secretary of State, 1949-50; Assistant Secretary of State, Far Eastern Affairs, 1950-51; Secretary of State, 1961-69; president, Rockefeller Foundation, 1952-60; Sibley Professor of International Law, University of Georgia, 1970- ; Legion of Merit; Phi Beta Kappa. (See also *Current Biography: July 1961.*)

SCHROEDER, PATRICIA (1940-). Born, Portland, Oregon; B.A., magna cum laude, University of Minnesota, 1961; J.D., Harvard Law School, 1964; field attorney, National Labor Relations Board, Denver, 1964-66; faculty member, Community College of Denver, 1969-70; University of Colorado, 1969- ; Regis College, 1970- ; hearing officer, Colorado Department of Personnel, 1971-72; legal counsel, Planned Parenthood of Colorado; member, US House of Representatives (Democrat, Colorado), 1972- ; Phi Beta Kappa.

STEINEM, GLORIA (1936-). Born, Toledo, Ohio; B.A., magna cum laude, Smith College, 1956; Chester Bowles Asian fellow, University of Delhi and University of Calcutta, 1956-58; contributing writer for *Esquire, Life, Harper's, Vogue, Glamour,* New York *Times, McCall's, Ladies' Home Journal, Show, Look,* 1961- ; writer for weekly television show, "That Was the Week That Was," NBC, 1964-65; contributing editor, *New York* magazine; editor, *MS.* magazine, 1972- ; Phi Beta Kappa; author, *The Thousand Indians,* 1957; *The Beach Book,* 1963. (See also *Current Biography: March 1972.*)

CUMULATIVE AUTHOR INDEX

1970-1971—1972-1973

A cumulative author index to the volumes of REPRESENTATIVE AMERICAN SPEECHES for the years 1937-1938 through 1959-1960 appears in the 1959-1960 volume and for the years 1960-1961 through 1969-1970 in the 1969-1970 volume.

(6347)